To Leon [illegible]
With best wishes,
John Garrard

MIXAIL ČULKOV:
AN INTRODUCTION TO HIS PROSE AND VERSE

SLAVISTIC PRINTINGS AND REPRINTINGS

edited by

C. H. VAN SCHOONEVELD

Indiana University

CXVI

1970

MOUTON

THE HAGUE · PARIS

Bronze Plaque Designed for Culkov's Grave, Now in the Institute of Russian Literature, Leningrad.

MIXAIL ČULKOV

AN INTRODUCTION TO HIS PROSE AND VERSE

by

J. G. GARRARD

Dartmouth College

1970

MOUTON

THE HAGUE · PARIS

LIBRARY OF CONGRESS CATALOG CARD NUMBER: 70-134550

Printed in The Netherlands by Mouton & Co., Printers, The Hague.

To C., R., and S.

PREFACE

It is quite natural perhaps that in survey courses of Russian literature scant attention should be paid to the eighteenth century, and then only to half a dozen major figures. However, in the hop, skip and jump of such surveys many admittedly secondary, but nonetheless important, writers get ignored. Mixail Dmitrievič Čulkov is one of these unfortunates. His interest for us today is certainly more historical than intrinsic, and yet if we wish to acquire a thorough understanding of eighteenth-century Russian literature, it is only right and proper to devote some attention to such lesser figures. Two hundred years have passed since Čulkov was producing his works in prose and verse; it seems appropriate that at long last a monograph should be given over to a discussion of their chief features and merits. In the cultural terrain of any given century the peaks may be the most clearly visible, but they are not the only topographical features worth examining. There comes a time when one must doff one's seven-league boots and take a more leisurely walk through the foothills and valleys. Hence, I have tried to keep pretty close to sea level in this book. I have also tried to make its bulk commensurate with the size of Čulkov as a writer, thus avoiding the scholarly trend of larger and larger tomes about smaller and smaller topics, and not to overload Čulkov's works with the relative subtleties of modern criticism.

Čulkov's shoulders are a little too narrow to bear the full weight of a general discussion of Russian eighteenth-century literature during the reign of Catherine II, even though he was active in many fields. Nevertheless, the man was a part of his cultural environment and I have attempted to set his work against the backdrop of contemporary Russian literature and also as far as was possible to locate them in the broader context of European developments, particularly in prose fiction. This has entailed a certain amount of source-hunting, but I hope I have managed to avoid the worst sins of *Quellenforschung*. The literature of any nation in its organic development draws nourishment from both native and foreign sources. The 'mix' naturally varies from country to country and from period to period, but both native and foreign influences are normally present. If one or the other is absent for any length of time, a literature either stagnates or becomes superficial and imitative. Russian writers in the first half of the eighteenth century, notably Trediakovskij and Sumarokov, thought of their country as a very recent arrival on the European cultural stage; they expressed their delight that Apollo had finally consented to visit them and expressed great hopes for the future history of Russian literature, which was coming of age at the eleventh hour. No one would deny that foreign influences predominated at this period, although recent scholarship has taught us that they should not be exaggerated and that eighteenth-century Russian literature is no means entirely imitative: this much indeed emerges from a study of Čulkov's own career. However, I have preferred to pay more attention to the foreign influences, since I feel that they are of greater significance, and am content to have my colleagues in the Soviet Union, with their easier access to rare books and archival materials, concentrate their efforts on seeking the native sources of Čulkov's work.

This brings me to a final point regarding accessibility of material. Any scholar working in Russian eighteenth-century studies is plagued with the problem of locating rare works. If he finds certain works difficult to locate then so will his prospective readers; it therefore becomes necessary to outline the contents of these works from time to time in order to ensure that the argument can be followed. In the United States we are fortunate to have available the remarkable Judin collection of eighteenth-century Russian books in the Library of Congress, and yet for many items one is still obliged to consult the libraries of the Soviet Union, particularly the Saltykov-Ščedrin Public Library in Leningrad, the Library of the Academy of Sciences in Leningrad, and the Lenin Library in Moscow. I would like to express my thanks to the Humanities Fund, Inc. of New York City and the Research Committee of Dartmouth College for generous financial assistance which made it possible for me to work at these libraries. I am particularly grateful to M. M. Gurevič of the Library of the Academy of Sciences and also to the late P. N. Berkov and to G. N. Moiseeva of the Institute of Russian Literature (Puškinskij Dom) in Leningrad for their kindness, as well as to Dr. M. Widnäs of the Helsinki University Library.

This study of Čulkov's works started out as a doctoral thesis at

Columbia University. I am happy to acknowledge my debt to Professor Leon Stilman of the Department of Slavic Languages at Columbia, as well as to his colleagues Professors William E. Harkins and Robert A. Maguire. Dr. C. L. Drage of the School of Slavonic and East European Studies, University of London, read the entire manuscript and made many valuable suggestions for its improvement, and Dr. A. Pennington of Lady Margaret Hall, Oxford University, kindly helped with a number of linguistic problems. To my wife I owe the greatest debt, for her encouragement and cheerful support during the preparation of this study.

Portions of chapter V and chapters II and VI originally appeared as articles in the *Slavic Review* and the *Slavonic and East European Review,* and are reprinted here by kind permission of the editors of those journals.

Hanover, New Hampshire J. G. G.

CONTENTS

I

A JACK OF ALL TRADES

Mixail Čulkov's adult life spanned the greater part of the reign of Catherine II: he was born in 1743 and died in 1792.[1] This vitally important period in Russian cultural history witnessed the early growth of the first permanent Russian theater, the appearance of satirical journals, the development of literary parody, the first signs of dissatisfaction with neo-classical aesthetics, the extensive translation of French and other foreign novels, as well as the first attempts at original works of prose fiction (that is, in printed literature), and a lively interest in Russian history and folklore. In nearly all of these literary trends and events Čulkov played an active, and sometimes a leading, role. The standard Soviet history of Russian literature describes him as "novelist, poet, journalist, economist, collector of folklore, and for a number of years professional man of letters".[2]

Čulkov was nothing if not industrious. Apart from his works in prose fiction and verse, which are our immediate concern here, he produced a *Brief Mythological Lexicon*, which listed with explanations the deities of Classical antiquity and also some ancient Slavic pagan gods; the first printed collection of Russian folksongs; a very detailed and informative history of Russian commerce which appeared in several volumes from 1781 to 1788; a *Dictionary of Russian Superstitions,* and numerous other works, the last of which was a collection of Russian laws, completed by another hand after his death.[3] Students of Russian folklore and ethnography owe a debt to Čulkov, and his works

[1] A plaque designed for his gravestone and later presented by his descendants to the Russian Academy of Sciences states that Čulkov "lived 49 years" and "passed away (*predstavilsja*) in Moscow on October 24, 1792". This is quoted in *Iroikomičeskaja poèma*, ed. B. Tomaševskij (Leningrad, 1933), p. 181, and in V. Šklovskij, *Čulkov i Levšin* (Leningrad, 1933), pp. 88-89.

[2] *Istorija russkoj literatury*, IV (Moscow-Leningrad, 1947), 270.

[3] For a complete listing of all Čulkov's works, see the Bibliography at the end of this book.

on Russian commercial history are still regarded as valuable contributions written at a time when hardly anything was being done by way of serious research into this subject.

Čulkov was obviously well known to his contemporaries, but he does not appear to have attracted the attention of the writers of memoirs of this period. Our biographical information is consequently limited to the scattered comments, letters, and official documents that have been painstakingly assembled and collated by scholars since the mid-nineteenth century. Even these provide no evidence for Čulkov's earliest years, and the place of his birth remains unknown. Unfortunately for the literary historian, Čulkov was himself reticent about his past later in life when he had become a government official of some standing. However, in 1790, two years before his death, he did publish a list of his works preceded by a brief autobiographical sketch. In it he says simply that he studied at Moscow University in his youth (*v mladoletstve*) but did not complete his studies.[4] Moscow University, the first such institution of higher learning in Russia, was founded in 1755 largely as a result of the strenuous efforts and persistence of Mixail Lomonosov. Attached to the new university were two Gymnasia, one for members of the nobility, the other for 'non-nobles' or *raznočincy*.[5] From 1756 until 1758 (and possibly later) Čulkov was a student at the Gymnasium for non-nobles, at about the same time as Denis Fonvizin and Nikolaj Novikov were enrolled at the Gymnasium for the nobility. This is evidently what Čulkov meant by studying at Moscow University. Some of his school books have survived, including one with the following inscription in Latin: "Ann:D: 756 in Ann: 757 Sum ex libris Michaelis Czulkoff."[6] He seems to have been a good student, for the newspaper *Moscow News* (*Moskovskie vedomosti*) listed him in its

[4] Originally published in *Ekonomičeskie zapiski*, 2nd ed. (Moscow, 1790), the sketch is reproduced in *Iroi-komičeskaja poèma*, pp. 190-191.

[5] Serfs were explicitly excluded. The meaning of the word *raznočinec* has not remained constant, but at this period it meant simply any person who was not a member of the *dvorjanstvo*, that is, not a member of the landowning gentry or in the upper echelons of civilian or military service; see C. Becker, "*Raznochintsy:* The Development of the Word and of the Concept", *American Slavic and East European Review*, XVIII (1959), 67. See also Marc Raeff, *Origins of the Russian Intelligentsia: The Eighteenth-Century Nobility* (New York, 1966).

[6] A photograph of the inscription on a *Rhetoric*, presumably Lomonosov's, appears inside the back cover of *Sočinenija Mixaila Dmitrieviča Čulkova*, I (St. Petersburg, 1913). It is also quoted in *Iroi-komičeskaja poèma*, p. 184; but Tomaševskij incorrectly has "Sunt" for "Sum".

issue of May 12, 1758 as a student at the Gymnasium who had received an award for his school work.[7]

Čulkov's attendance at the Gymnasium for *raznočincy* indicates his social background: he was clearly not nobly born nor a member of the landed gentry. The Soviet scholar Grigorij Gukovskij has pointed out that the sons of merchants and particularly the sons of clerics seized eagerly the opportunities offered them by the opening of the non-noble Gymnasium at Moscow University.[8] These men also very often went into government civilian service following their studies, as Čulkov himself did. It seems reasonable to conclude that he came either from a merchant or clerical family.[9] Whichever was the case, he was a man of modest social background, and in a society with a fairly rigid class structure (an example of which is the foundation of two separate Gymnasia at Moscow University) and where social mobility was restricted, Čulkov's prospects could not have looked very bright. Given his poverty and lack of benefactors, one can more readily understand the bewildering variety of his publishing activities. He was prepared to attempt any and all ways of achieving fame and fortune as well as a measure of respectability. More will be said of this later.

Quite naturally, in seeking to learn something about Čulkov's early years and background Russian scholars have turned to his first works, doubtless on the assumption that a young author usually puts more of himself in his first works than in any others. The temptation is doubly strong in the case of Čulkov because much of his early work was written in the first person, for example his journal *This and That* (*I to i së*), which appeared in 1769.[10] In the second issue of this weekly publication Čulkov tells the story of a boy who studied hard, read church books, but was sorely beaten by his miserly father when he asked for a tutor. Then he admits: "I had almost the same fate as this thrashed

[7] *Čulkov i Levšin*, p. 61.

[8] Gr. Gukovskij, *Očerki po istorii russkoj literatury XVIII veka. Dvorjanskaja fronda v literature 1750-x–1750-x godov* (Moscow-Leningrad, 1936), p. 28.

[9] Ju. Sokolov in his standard work *Russian Folklore* (New York, 1950), p. 559 refers to Čulkov as 'the son of a court stove tender'. This almost certainly results from a confusion with another Čulkov; Sokolov may have been drawing upon the brief biographical sketches in the preliminary lists for the *Russkij biografičeskij slovar'* in *Sbornik imp. russkogo istoričeskogo obščestva*, Vol. 62 (St. Petersburg, 1888), p. 428, col. 1. Čulkov should not of course be confused either with the Freemason V. V. Čulkov, a member of Novikov's circle and financial supporter of the "Družeskoe učënoe obščestvo", as has been done by Professor A. McConnell in his book *A Russian* Philosophe *Alexander Radishchev, 1749-1802* (The Hague, 1964), p. 64.

[10] *I to i së* (St. Petersburg, 1769).

young lad. My father was more of a money-grubber than his and rewarded me so handsomely with rod and lash that I am ashamed to admit it . . .". He continues the story and relates how the boy, becoming desperate, stole money from his father and left Moscow for Kiev, where he studied under a tutor and learned many languages. It is possible that there is something of Čulkov's own past in this story, but clearly we are here in the realm of speculation, and furthermore in the following issue of the journal Čulkov himself warns his readers that "not everything that I say about myself will be true and sometimes while talking about myself I shall be referring to someone else".[11] Čulkov seems to have enjoyed mystification. In Week 42 of *This and That* he announces: "I grew up in the city in which I was born, and was born where I was brought up." [12]

Further study of archival material by Russian scholars may help us determine when Čulkov left the Gymnasium at Moscow University. At present we can say with assurance only that he was still there as late as the spring of 1758. This leaves us with a gap of three years until 1761 when, according to his own account, he became a court actor, having moved from Moscow to St. Petersburg.[13] Čulkov may have first become interested in the theater while still at school in Moscow, because it would appear that a theatrical school was established there at the University soon after its foundation as a result of the enthusiasm of Mixail Xeraskov, later Director of the Moscow University and a prolific writer in the neo-classical tradition. Students were encouraged to join the theatrical school, and the Moscow newspaper *Moskovskie vedomosti* in June and July of 1757 invited the participation of female performers, thus paralleling a similar invitation made by Aleksandr Sumarokov, then director of the newly established permanent Russian court theater in St. Petersburg. The nineteenth-century scholar I. E. Zabelin, who wrote a number of studies on the early history of Moscow, discovered that eighteen students of the 'non-noble' Gymnasium

[11] Indeed, the story may be a reference to Čulkov's chief literary foe, Fëdor Èmin, who was accused of going to Kiev and then returning to St. Petersburg pretending to be an aristocrat from Istanbul. On the polemic between Čulkov and Èmin, see Chapter III.

[12] "Ja vzros v tom gorode v kotorom rodilsja, a rodilsja tut, gde i vospitan." For Šklovskij this is sufficient to indicate that Čulkov was born in Moscow. See: *Čulkov i Levšin*, p. 60.

[13] In a letter dated January 27, 1765 Čulkov requested permission to leave the theater and become a lackey. In the course of the letter he said that he had been an actor for three years and ten months. This letter, together with other documents relating to the request, is quoted by Šklovskij, pp. 61-64.

in fact formed a regular troupe.[14] It seems very likely that Čulkov was one of this troupe before he left the Gymnasium. Some young actors were transferred from Moscow to the court theater in 1761 and once again this appears to dovetail with what we already know of Čulkov's acting career.

It is important to dispel the myth of Čulkov's membership in the original troupe established by Fëdor Volkov in Jaroslavl' in 1750. It seems to be traceable to inaccurate secondhand accounts by nineteenth-century writers on the early Russian theater, most of them based upon conversations with the famous actor Ivan Dmitrevskij. Dmitrevskij, who died in 1821, was one of the original members of Volkov's troupe, and later established himself as the leading actor of his day. Naturally, he must be regarded as an important source, but the later nineteenth-century accounts of what he is supposed to have said or written about the eighteenth-century theater contain obvious inaccuracies. In 1953 the Academy of Sciences published a collection of documents entitled *F. G. Volkov and the Russian Theatre of his Time* (*F. G. Volkov i russkij teatr ego vremeni*). From these materials we learn that when Volkov was summoned to the capital by the Empress Elizabeth in January of 1752 he left Jaroslavl' with ten men. Čulkov was not one of them. The Empress was apparently not overly impressed by the troupe, in particular by its repertoire, and she disbanded it in the summer of 1752. However, four of the aspiring actors were placed in the aristocratic Cadet School (*Suxoputnyj šljaxetnyj kadeckij korpus*) in order to study and acquire some polish and then in January of 1755 brought back to the court to prepare a repertoire under the direction of Aleksandr Sumarokov. An imperial decree of August 30 the following year established the first permanent Russian theater. In all these documents we find not a single reference to Mixail Čulkov.[15]

If we can now say with some assurance that Čulkov was a court

[14] Quoted by V. V. Kallaš and N. E. Èfros in their *Istorija russkogo teatra*, I (Moscow, 1914), 115. See also on these developments V. Vsevolodskij-Gerngross, *Russkij teatr. Ot istokov do serediny XVIII veka* (Moscow, 1957), pp. 235-238.

[15] The myth has persisted with surprising stubbornness and is repeated by Boris Tomaševskij in *Iroi-komičeskaja poèma*. He argues that Čulkov was one of the original members of Volkov's troupe and that he could not have been born as late as 1743 since this would have made him only seven years old in 1750 when the troupe began to give performances. This also leads him to suggest that Čulkov was born in Jaroslavl'. In fact Čulkov has been claimed as one of the honored sons of that city and is listed as such in at least two biblographical studies: S. A. Zolotarëv, *Pisateli-jaroslavcy* (Jaroslavl', 1920) and N. G. Ogurcov, *Dejateli jaroslavskogo kraja. Opyt mestnoj bibliografii* (Jaroslavl', 1924).

actor in St. Petersburg in 1765, we are still confronted by some problems regarding his actual activities during the preceding three or four years. In a vaudeville by Šaxovskoj, supposedly based upon the oral memoirs of the actor Ivan Dmitrevskij and entitled "Fëdor Volkov or the Birthday of the Russian Theater" ("Fëdor Volkov ili den' roždenija russkogo teatra"), Čulkov was portrayed as a young seminarian whose function in the new theater was to dress wigs and beards for the performers. This vaudeville, immensely popular around 1840, belongs with numerous other accounts which traced their source to Dmitrevskij, and like them it is obviously not a piece of reliable evidence: we know, for example, that Čulkov was not a member of Volkov's troupe. But our curiosity is bound to be aroused by the suggestion that Čulkov was a young seminarian and prepared wigs and beards. In the first place, we have already noted that he might well have been the son of a priest, and secondly, he is referred to as a 'court barber' (*Hofbarbier*) by the anonymous author of a list of forty-two noteworthy Russian authors of the century both living and dead, which was published in 1768 in a Leipzig journal.[16] The tone of this biographical note is rather condescending, and calling Čulkov a barber may have been intended as an insult by the anonymous author: this is the view of several Russian scholars. However, there is very little point in calling a rising young author, whatever his social origin, a court barber if he is not and has never been one. There are in fact three references to barbers in the early issues of Čulkov's journal *This and That*. One must of course always be wary of the dangers of 'internal evidence', yet there seems good reason to believe that Čulkov was here reacting to the note in "Nachricht von einigen russischen Schriftstellern", which had appeared only a few months earlier in 1768. In the very first January issue of the journal he writes:

I love to chatter, but I don't have the gift of amusing people intelligently, and this is because I am not as clever as others. However, a good man has promised to give me some instruction and now it is simply a matter of arranging with him how much he will take per month for his lessons. He is a grown man and an extremely skillful barber (*Parikmaxer*); he can comb hair

[16] "Nachricht von einigen russischen Schriftstellern, nebst einen kurzen Berichte vom russischen Theater." The brief biographical notes have been attributed to various authors, including Dmitrevskij and Vladimir Lukin. The arguments in favor of A. A. Volkov presented by P. N. Berkov in *Izvestija Ak. Nauk. Otd. Obšč. nauk*, No. 8 (1931), 937-952, seem to have found wide acceptance. The notes are reproduced by P. A. Efremov in his *Materialy dlja istorii russkoj literatury* (St. Petersburg, 1867), pp. 145-160.

without the slightest mistake and says that he has an inborn talent for it. He once assured me that literature is worth far less than the art of curling hair (*slovesnye nauki gorazdo men'še stojat, neželi volosopodvivatel'noe iskus-svto*).

At the end of Week 2 of the journal Čulkov announces that he has decided to become a barber (or hairdresser) and mentions some of the new wig styles he has in mind. At the beginning of Week 4 he declares he is glad that he has a barber as a teacher. He has ordered himself a fine ivory comb with which he intends to "comb the hair of the whole town and its suburbs, that is, of those people who are very negligent and do not take care of their appearance".

These references to the profession of hairdressing occur only in the January issues of the journal and seem to be Čulkov's response to the author of "Nachricht von einigen russischen Schriftstellern", who had preferred to call him a court barber instead of a court actor – the note contains no mention of Čulkov's acting career. If this is a correct interpretation of the scanty evidence that is available to us, then we can say that Čulkov joined the budding Russian court theater as a barber in charge of wigs and beards rather than as an actor, but later graduated to acting.

The only surviving eye-witness account of his acting is far from complimentary. It is a verse epigram written by the actor Ivan Sokolov on Čulkov's tearful performance in the tragedy "Sinav and Truvor" by Sumarokov.[17] He certainly does not seem to have made his mark as an actor, although once again there is not much evidence concerning his acting ability and the parts he played. The only evidence we have, in fact, is an alleged partial copy of a history of the Russian theater written by Ivan Dmitrevskij, which has not survived in the original. However, what is purported to be a copy of the manuscript by an actor Ivan Nosov has survived and was first published in 1883.[18] It is entitled "Chronicle of the Russian Theater" and consists of a series of dated entries listing theatrical performances given in Russia from the middle of the seventeenth century, often including the author or translator of

[17] Quoted in *Iroi-komičeskaja poèma*, p. 184. Tomaševskij quotes Čulkov's equally biting reply to Sokolov, also in verse.

[18] "Xronika russkogo teatra", *Čtenija v imp. Obščestve istorii i drevnostej rossijskix pri Mosk. universitete*, Vols. 121, 122 (1882). Without quoting sources V. Vsevolodskij-Gerngross states that "It is possible that in Moscow he took part in Volkov's mascarade 'Minerva Triumphant.' He is known to have played only one role, the messenger in the tragedy 'Xorev'. Čulkov was handsome, but too tall, and this evidently made it difficult for him to pursue an acting career." See his *Russkij teatr vtoroj poloviny XVIII veka* (Moscow, 1960), p. 112.

the play in question and the names of the performers. Only certain years have entries and there are frequent and lengthy gaps. The text comes to an end at the year 1784. It contains many errors and must be approached with caution. However, since it does refer to Čulkov, it seems worthwhile examining what it has to say about his activities as both actor and playwright.

According to Nosov's account, both Čulkov and his friend and literary collaborator Mixail Popov appeared three times in performances at Jaroslavl' in 1751 (the text has no entries for 1750). To celebrate the Empress' birthday, a comedy by Fëdor Volkov was presented with Čulkov acting the part of a Jaroslavl' merchant and Popov his wife.[19] From the year 1751 the "Chronicle" jumps to 1757. Čulkov is said to have appeared at the Imperial Theater three times in this year, first as Vissarion in Sumarokov's one-act verse drama "The Hermit" ("Pustynnik"), secondly, also in February, as Vitozar in Sumarokov's "Semira", and lastly in June as the Baron in "The Meditative Man" ("Razdumčivyj"), supposedly translated from a French play by Destouches (*Le Philosophe marié*?). According to the "Chronicle" in 1758 Čulkov played Angélique's father in a Russian version of Molière's *George Dandin*, and then in January of 1759 he appeared as 'first soldier' in a performance of *Richard III* given at the Winter Palace. Finally, in 1763 he is alleged to have performed in Dmitrevskij's translation of Molière's *L'Amour médecin*.[20]

The facts of the matter are that Čulkov's acting career lasted from 1761 until 1765, so the listing of his performances in Nosov's "Chronicle" both begins and ends too early, although it certainly does overlap with his career. Čulkov may well have appeared in some, if not all, of the roles allotted to him in the "Chronicle", but not in the years indicated. The first thing that strikes one about the parts Čulkov is alleged to have played is that they are by no means leading roles. Judging from the "Chronicle" – and it is all we have – Čulkov specialized in supporting roles, and even walk-on parts in the case of *Richard III*. This may explain why he did not attract the attention of his contemporaries as an actor. Presumably, the realization that his acting ability was limited prompted Čulkov to request permission to leave the court

[19] "Xronika", Vol. 121, 94. The inclusion of Mixail Popov is an obvious error, due to a confusion in first names: official documents show that an Aleksej Popov and a Jakov Popov were among the group of ten actors who accompanied Volkov from Jaroslavl' to St. Petersburg.

[20] For these references to Čulkov see Vol. 121, pp. 97, 98, 105, 121, and 141-142; Vol. 122, p. 261.

theater in 1765 after nearly four years of association with the troupe. There may also have been a more homely reason for his decision. Čulkov must have got married at about this time and his son Vladimir was born in 1766.[21] No doubt these new family responsibilities impressed upon him the necessity of switching to a steadier, if more mundane, career which would guarantee him a regular income.

Before leaving Nosov's "Chronicle" we must note that it mentions Čulkov as playwright as well as actor. Here, as elsewhere, the information provided is almost certainly a mixture of fact and fiction, blurred by copyists' errors. According to the "Chronicle" on January 10, 1763 the court actors at the Moscow Theater gave a performance of "Saint's Day, or They Came to Dinner, But Found the Door Locked in Their Faces" ("Imeninnik, ili prišli na obed, da zamku poklonilis'"), a comedy in two acts by "M. Ču".[22] The names of the characters in this play are Russian and provide quite a striking contrast to the Greek, Roman, and Oriental names in most of the plays performed at that time. The famous comic actor Jakov Šumskij, who was one of the original members of Volkov's troupe, is said to have played the part of a Vologda merchant named Karp Petrovič. Later in 1763 the court actors at the Winter Palace gave the first performance of "O Times! O Age! And This is Man!" ("O vremena! o vek! i èto čelovek!"), a comedy in four acts in prose by "M. Č." [23] Čulkov himself also appeared in this play. Finally, under an entry for January 9, 1779, we read that at the court theater in St. Petersburg a performance of "Polyeuctus, or Call It What You Will" ("Polièvkt ili kak xočeš' nazovi") was given. It is called a 'comedy in two acts in prose, by the actor Mix. Čulkov'.[24]

Čulkov's authorship of the first two plays has not been corroborated by other evidence; neither has survived. The last play, however, is mentioned by the anonymous author of "Nachricht von einigen russischen Schriftstellern" as having been written by Čulkov; Nikolaj Novikov also lists it among Čulkov's works in his *Attempt at an Historical Dictionary of Russian Writers* which was published shortly

[21] A. Fomin, "K biografii M. D. Čulkova (Rod. 1740 g.-um. 1793 g.)," *Knigovedenie*, No. 7-8 (1894), p. 16. Fomin discovered some documents relating to Čulkov in the archives of the Moscow Assembly of Nobles' Deputies. One was a *semejnyj list* dated August 4, 1785 stating that Čulkov had married Anna, daughter of a district police-officer (*kommissar*) named Gavrila Ivanovič Batalin, and that in 1766 a son had been born to the couple.

[22] "Xronika", Vol. 121, p. 228.

[23] *Ibid.*, Vol. 122, p. 282.

[24] *Ibid.*, Vol. 122, p. 324.

afterwards in 1772.[25] Čulkov himself in a brief autobiographical sketch, which he published towards the end of his life in 1790 partially to correct and amplify Novikov's note, mentions the play "Kak xočeš' nazovi" and a second play that remained unfinished: "Negligent But Virtuous" ("Dobrodel'no neradivyj"). Of the first play he notes that it was played at the court theater 'repeatedly' (*neodnokratno*).[26] The play has in fact survived in an actor's copy made in 1783 and was first published in the series *Literary Heritage* in 1933.[27]

"Call It What You Will" is indeed written in prose, as the "Chronicle" says, but has only one act, divided into fourteen scenes, at least in the actor's copy of 1783. The scenes often amount to no more than a brief speech by one or another character. The plot is very familiar: the parents of the heroine Euthymia each have made their own choice for her husband, but she herself prefers Polyeuctus. Kirjak the father's servant resolves to interfere, for no apparent reason except from the goodness of his heart, and manages very successfully, in the manner of the wily servant familiar in French comedy, to make the two rival suitors appear ridiculous in the presence of the parents, who then gracefully agree to give their blessing to the immediate marriage of their daughter and Polyeuctus. The Classical names of the characters contrast with their down-to-earth speech, which is very colloquial, at times even vulgar, as in the verbal clashes between the father and mother. If the plot reminds us of French comedy, there are still some features of the play that are specifically Russian in nature, both as regards language and situation. Čulkov soon reveals his fondness for proverbs; for example, Artemon the father taunts his wife during one of their verbal exchanges: "A woman has long hair, but her intelligence does not reach far" (*U baby volos dolog, da um korotok*). Artemon also threatens to forget himself and beat his wife, employing the 'ancient methods'. This

[25] Nikolaj Novikov, *Opyt istoričeskogo slovarja o rossijskix pisateljax* (St. Petersburg, 1772), pp. 243-244. This work has been republished by P. A. Efremov in his *Materialy dlja istorii russkoj literatury* (St. Petersburg, 1867) and more recently in *Izbrannye sočinenija N. I. Novikova* (Moscow-Leningrad, 1951).

[26] This sketch, which is for the most part a listing of works by Čulkov both published and unpublished, appeared in the second edition of his *Ekonomičeskie zapiski* (Moscow, 1790). Čulkov makes no mention of his acting career, probably regarding it as an unfortunate episode in his life that was best forgotten. The sketch has been reproduced by Tomaševskij in *Iroi-komičeskaja poèma*, pp. 190-191.

[27] *Literaturnoe nasledstvo*, No. 9-10 (Moscow, 1933), pp. 222-242. N. Xardžiev, who assisted Šklovskij in collecting material for his book *Čulkov i Levšin*, provides a brief introduction.

sounds like an echo of the tyrannical behavior counselled in the sixteenth-century Muscovite *Book of Household Management* (*Domostroj*).

Čulkov's comedy is an example of the Russification of an international plot that can be traced back to the comedies of Menander, Plautus and Terence. It contains the stereotyped figures of the parents, the young lovers, the distasteful suitors – dupes of the typical shrewd valet, who plays a catalytic role in the action. It is a bourgeois play which portrays men and women of the Russian middle class. The father Artemon is described by Čulkov as 'a noble of modest means' (*nebogatyj dvorjanin*). "Call It What You Will" tells the familiar story of young love triumphant and ends with wedding bells. Its considerable popularity with the theater-going public illustrates the growing taste of an expanding audience for this type of comedy during the reign of Catherine II. It offers a notable contrast to the pompous and heavy-handed tragedies of Sumarokov, and also to his comedies, which contain far more social satire; Sumarokov sought to teach in both his tragedies and his comedies. There is no 'message' in Čulkov's comedy.

The author of "Nachricht von einigen russischen Schriftstellern" asserts that Čulkov's play "soll eine schwache Critik über des Hrn. Lukin seine Comödie seyn". This suggests that in the opinion of some people at least Čulkov had written a parody of a play by Vladimir Lukin, the author of numerous translations and adaptations of French plays that were quite popular during the sixties. N. Xardžiev, in his introduction to the text of Čulkov's play, points out that it bears a resemblance to Lukin's comedy "The Windbag" ("Pustomelja"), although it seems to contain no parodical elements. Lukin's comedy is a free adaptation (partly a translation) of *Le Babillard* (1725) by Louis de Boissy. There is no reason why Čulkov should not have independently adapted the same play while he was associated with the court theater in the early sixties.[28] The play offers an illustration of Čulkov's outlook on literature and the type of material he was prepared to turn his hand to. It also indicates that he was not original; like so many Russian authors of the time he imitated and adapted. Hence the constant accusations and counter-accusations of plagiarism that abound in literary polemic at this period.

Čulkov's request of January 27, 1765 that he be permitted to leave the court theater met with a prompt and favorable reply and in the

[28] "Pustomelja" first appeared in V. Lukin, *Sočinenii i perevody* (St. Petersburg, 1765). It is of course possible that the play was known shortly before in manuscript.

following month we find him officially registered as a court lackey (*pridvornyj lakej*) with a salary of forty rubles a year.[29] During the next two years Čulkov changed jobs quite rapidly. At the same time he started to publish works of varied content, obviously in an attempt to make his mark in the cultural life of St. Petersburg. He still held his position of court lackey at the beginning of 1766, as we can tell from a letter dated February 1 in which he requested that the Academy print the first part of his collection of tales entitled *The Mocker, or Slavic Tales* (*Peresmešnik, ili slavenskie skazki*).[30] But in a document reporting the printing of this volume dated November 3, 1766, Čulkov is referred to as a 'retired lackey'.[31] The following February Čulkov addressed a second request to the Academy to publish six hundred copies of his *Brief Mythological Lexicon* (*Kratkoj mifologičeskoj leksikon*) and this time signed himself 'court quartermaster' (*pridvornyj kvartirmejster*).[32] When this last work was published later in 1767, it was dedicated formally to Vasilij Il'ič Bibikov, director of the court theater. The *Lexicon* was a work of some substance, providing a useful list (hitherto unavailable in Russian in such detail) of the major figures in Classical mythology and also of some of the Slavic gods, for example, Dažbog.[33] In his Foreword Čulkov wrote in part: "I undertook to compile this brief lexicon with the aim of being of service to those of my compatriots who do not know foreign languages." The fact that Bibikov permitted the *Lexicon* to be dedicated to him shows that Čulkov's departure from the court theater was not occasioned by any ill-feeling on the part of the authorities.

Čulkov continued his writing career and in 1768 further parts of his collection *The Mocker, or Slavic Tales* were published. He may have continued to serve at court, although we have no information as to his

[29] *Čulkov i Levšin,* p. 63. Šklovskij quotes the document signed by Prince Nikolaj Golicyn announcing that the Empress had graciously granted Čulkov's request.

[30] Čulkov signs himself "court lackey". See: V. P. Semennikov, *Materialy dlja istorii russkoj literatury i dlja slovarja pisatelej èpoxi Ekateriny II* (St. Petersburg, 1914), p. 132. This work appeared as a supplement to the journal *Russkij Bibliofil.*

[31] *Loc. cit.*

[32] *Ibid.*, p. 133. Presumably this is a higher position – "lackey" being at the bottom of the ladder in court service. I have been unable to discover precisely what duties a "quartermaster" performed.

[33] Both Čulkov and his friend Popov shared an interest in Slavic pagan mythology and Russian folklore. In the foreword to his *Opisanie drevnego slavenskogo jazyčeskogo basnoslovija* (St. Petersburg, 1768) Popov mentioned the sources upon which we may presume both drew: the ancient chronicles, the historical works of Lomonosov, and also popular Russian tales, songs, games, and customs.

activities at this time. We know only that he went on publishing works of a varied character at regular intervals.[34] Prolific as he was, he appeared to make little or no profit from his publications. Šklovskij quotes a document from the archives of the Academy of Sciences proving that in 1770 Čulkov had still not paid for the printing of his *Lexicon* three years earlier.[35] This fact illustrates the second crucial feature in Čulkov's situation, which follows naturally from the first, his modest social background. Čulkov was poor and tried to earn a living as a professional man of letters. In this attempt he failed, as he was almost bound to, because without generous patronage a writer at that period in Russia could hardly hope to survive; this was still an age when diamond-studded snuffboxes were awarded for a flattering ode. Čulkov also assayed this route to success. He wrote in 1767 an "Ode to His Imperial Highness, Heir to the Throne, Prince Pavel Petrovič, on the New Year". A manuscript copy of this ode, apparently the only copy in existence, is located in the Slavic collection of the University of Helsinki.[36] It is a typical panegyric ode written in inflated style, praising with cosmic imagery both Catherine and her son Paul. Čulkov may well have received a handsome gift for his efforts in the shape of a snuffbox. He certainly seems to have been rewarded with such a gift from Catherine in the early eighties for his history of Russian commerce, as we shall see later.

Even at the beginning of the nineteenth century Russian writers, for example Karamzin, were still receiving such marks of favor from the court. In his study of the writing profession in Russia the French scholar André Meynieux states: "En résume, et malgré l'opinion con-

[34] These brought him into contact with the literary figures of the day, including Sumarokov. V. P. Semennikov, in his *Russkie satiričeskie žurnaly 1769-1744 gg. Razyskanija ob izdateljax ix i sotrudnikax* (St. Petersburg, 1914), p. 17, quotes a letter from Sumarokov to G. V. Kozickij, private secretary to the Empress Catherine, in which he mentions waiting to discuss some matter of a translation with Čulkov. The letter is dated August 14, 1768.

[35] *Čulkov i Levšin*, p. 70. The Academy in fact seems to have made no effort to sell the books it published; they simply gathered dust in storage.

[36] "Oda Ego Imperatorskomu Vysočestvu Naslednomu Gosudarju Cesareviču Pavlu Petroviču na Novyj God, kotoruju prinosit vsepoddannejšyj rab Mixajlo Čulkov. 1768 Goda, Janvarja v I den'." Čulkov does not include this ode in his list of 1790 and no reference has ever been made to it in any published work that I am aware of. The ode apparently formed part of a manuscript library collected for Paul by the Empress Catherine. Part of the library came into the possession of Helsinki University through the generosity of an illegitimate son of the Grand Duke Constantine, elder brother of Tsar Nicholas I. See M. Widnäs, "La constitution du Fonds Slave de la Bibliothèque de Helsinki", *Cahiers du monde russe et soviétque*, II (Paris, 1961), 395-408.

traire des historiens de la littérature russe, il ne nous semble pas qu'on puisse vraiment parler de la littérature professionnelle en Russie avant Pouchkine . . .".[37] One must certainly bear in mind this peculiarity of the would-be professional writer's predicament in eighteenth-century Russia. It perhaps explains why in the satire against bad poets in Čulkov's second satirical journal *The Parnassian Trinket Dealer* (*Parnasskij ščepetil'nik*, 1770) the poets are to be auctioned off to the highest bidder. The theme of the bad poet is linked with a second significant theme in his work, that of money: what might be termed the commercial motif. The theme of buying and selling in Čulkov's first journal *This and That* has been remarked upon by the Soviet scholar A. V. Zapadov.[38] He points out that the theme of money was not unusual in the works of other writers of non-noble origin, such as Èmin, Vasilij Ruban (who contributed to *The Parnassian Trinket Dealer*), and Nikolaj Kurganov, the author of *Pis'movnik* (1769), a collection of tales, riddles and other material of a popular character. Men in Čulkov's modest situation would naturally be most concerned with money, and it is only to be expected that the commercial motif is frequently linked with the profession of writing in Čulkov's works.

Some uses of the commercial motif have strong autobiographical overtones in Čulkov's case. He prefaces the first of his three burlesque poems in 1769 with the remark that he wants to be happy and to have money; he has so far been unsuccessful obtaining money with his prose, and he now intends to try verse: "I was an impoverished prose writer, now I am going to try to make a living as a poet" (*This and That*, Week 16). A similar biographical interpretation might be placed upon the recurring references to other occupations, which are compared in their financial rewards to that of the professional writer, to the detriment of the latter. For example, we noted that the references to the hairdressing profession in the early issues of *This and That* were probably a response to the unfavorable mention he had been given the previous year in the "Nachricht von einigen russischen Schriftstellern", and Čulkov may have been a hairdresser himself. However, one can examine such references from a different viewpoint and pay particular attention to the statement of the skillful hairdresser who has offered to give Čulkov some instruction.

[37] André Meynieux, *La littérature et le métier d'écrivain en Russie avant Pouchkine* (Paris, 1966), p. 85. The contrary view had been expressed most fully by a group of Soviet scholars in the late twenties: T. Gric, V. Trenin, and M. Nikitin, *Slovesnost' i kommercija (Knižnaja lavka A. F. Smirdina)* (Moscow, 1929).

[38] A. V. Zapadov, "Žurnal M. D. Čulkova *I to i së* i ego literaturnoe okruženie", *XVIII vek*, No. 2 (Moscow-Leningrad, 1940), p. 97.

In the very first issue of the journal the hairdresser asserts that his profession is more worthy than literature. Čulkov says he is tempted to become a hairdresser because it pays well. More pointed is the episode with the foreign tailor that is related in Week 24 of *This and That*.

The tailor is a foreigner and had been a teacher of literature in his own country – he declines to say which.[39] Finding this occupation not sufficiently lucrative, he had decided to travel to Russia and become a 'French' tailor, since he was told that they were especially prized in that country. He advises Čulkov to give up his attempt to become a writer and instead become his apprentice, assuring him that he will earn more in a month as a tailor's apprentice than he does in a whole year as a writer.

Čulkov went out of his way to make the point that writers write for money, and he was apparently exasperated by the pomposity and hypocrisy of some of his contemporaries. In the second of his burlesque poems published in *This and That*, Čulkov digresses for a moment from his description of the popular holiday to say: "My pen is for sale: A kopek for a madrigal, a quarter-kopek for an epigram." [40] He gives his price list for various verse genres and says that he sells odes cheapest of all: they are without exception absolute rubbish, but they do find a very ready market. He had thought of writing tragedies but was frightened from this undertaking by a nightmare. He has written a comedy but hesitates to put it up for sale. It is important to note that one of the faults held against the bombastic and boastful Poet in another of the poems "The Poets' Sad Downfall" ("Plačevnoe padenie stixotvorcev") was his great wealth, which he had obtained from his writings. The Poet is unperturbed by the negative reaction to his works on Parnassus and declares: "I am wealthy through verse, I have acquired a house with my prose, With my satires I purchased a carriage with glass windows, With my novels I have raised myself up high, And spread my fame far and wide." [41] Such comments as this on the wealth that an opponent (here, Èmin) has supposedly acquired through his writings undoubtedly have personal overtones and indicate Čulkov's

[39] In the following issue of *This and That* Čulkov published a letter from the tailor signed "Bilgidpildon", a name that would not be out of place in *Gulliver's Travels*.

[40] *Poèty XVIII veka*, ed. G. P. Makogonenko and I. Z. Serman, vol. I (Leningrad, 1958), p. 436. These poems are more fully discussed in Chapter III.

[41] *Ibid.*, p. 468.

anger and also his concern at his own failure to become equally successful by acquiring the favor of generous patrons.

While the use of the commercial motif no doubt results from Čulkov's personal situation and his natural concern with money, its appearance in his works has broader implications. It illustrates the changes taking place in Russian literature during this period: namely, the introduction of mundane matters in areas from which they had formerly been excluded. The commercial motif introduces a sense of reality into literature – particularly important in the novel genre.

The commercial motif, sometimes amounting to no more than the simple mention of certain sums of money (although this is not without importance), appeared in Čulkov's works from the very first. Money is of course quite often mentioned in the tales narrated by the monk in *The Mocker*. The pursuit of money and the delights that it can purchase are the subject of several tales. In "The Magnanimous Cuckold" ("Velikodušnyj rogonosec") a servant steals a large amount of money and transforms himself into a dandy and gallant. "The Tale of the Origin of the Taffeta Beauty Spot" ("Skazka o roždenii taftjanoj muški") is in large part concerned with the pursuit of money. The impoverished student Neox, by means of cunning and a fair amount of skullduggery, finally manages to become rich and successful. He is the familiar hero of much bourgeois fiction who rises socially and also becomes wealthy at the end of the story or novel.

A good illustration of the possible uses to which the commercial motif might be put occurs in this same long tale narrated by the monk. When Neox arrives in the city of Vineta seeking fame and fortune, he is penniless and soon finds himself among a group of beggars, thieves, and prostitutes. A woman arranges for him to become the gigolo of a merchant's wife. Neox finds it hard to understand the wife at first because she talks in a strange way, quite unlike the fashionable young ladies with whom he had been consorting previously. However, they manage to come to terms; they strike a bargain whereby the woman agrees to pay for Neox's amorous attentions.[42] The episode is related with tongue in cheek and the use of much mercantile terminology: love is a business deal. In this case the commercial motif is quite appropriately introduced and at the same time serves to emphasize the humor of the situation and to hint at its passionless, cold-blooded atmosphere.

It is not hard to find similar uses of mercantile language in Čulkov's novel *The Comely Cook* (*Prigožaja povarixa,* 1770), in which the

[42] *Peresmešnik,* IV, 217-218.

commercial motif is woven into the very fabric of the narrative. At the beginning of the novel Martona is left alone and penniless, and after a very brief struggle with her conscience, she decides to make a living by selling the only wares that she possesses. The question of payment is of course the essential factor in all her relations with the various men she meets during the course of her adventures.

As early as December, 1769 Čulkov seems to have begun to realize that his publishing activities were not going to bring him sufficient income and furthermore that he might not be able to make a living as a writer. In Week 48 of his journal *This and That* he makes a revealing comment about himself and his situation:

> It was an unhappy day when I began to study in order to become in time a writer, not realizing that with this honorable title I would have to taste the bitter fruits of poverty. "Excellent writer" is a flattering and pleasant-sounding title, but quite often from this golden vessel we have to eat wormwood and not sweet food. Society behaves graciously towards us, accepts our works, forgives our weaknesses, and praises us according to our deserts, and this praise rejoices our vain thoughts. But should a writer, even in ignorance, have the misfortune to sin against the desires and wishes of his readers, then that small cloud of praise turns into a vast thundercloud of abuse and scorn for the writer.

It may be that some event called forth this complaint. In his final issue (Weeks 51 and 52 combined) Čulkov makes oblique references to his problems. He mentions that he has been mingling with 'the wise' and had earned their anger, but managed to find a corner in which to hide until the storm passed. Then he repeats that he had sought only to entertain in his journal. Soviet scholars may be correct in assuming that Čulkov had got himself into trouble with the Empress because of his outspokenness and was trying to hint at the reason for the closing of his journal. Čulkov's complaint in Week 48 still retains its interest insofar as it applies to his predicament and that of all would-be professional writers without independent means during this period. The whole of this issue has an unusually serious tone, which would indicate that Čulkov had for a moment removed his mask and was speaking about himself. In his early youth he seems to have been carried away by the idea of being a great and respected author, and so decided to devote all his energies to that end. Now he had been brought face to face with the brutal, if obvious, fact that a writer depends upon his audience, upon 'society' and its whims, unless he has some other source of income. At that time in Russia one had either to write as a hobby or elegant pastime, or else one was obliged to produce works to order and consider carefully the taste of wealthy patrons.

Čulkov digresses to discuss the effects of poverty:

> Evil misfortune suppresses virtue, and poverty, born of troubles and ill luck, leads a man not only to base and bad acts but also to sins. Many people believe that this is only the case with cowards and those who do not heed the voice of reason, but I have seen many poor people and not one of them was magnanimous, and I would think it most strange and wonderful if a man standing on a high mountain could shelter himself from the winds that blew against him fiercely from all sides.

Here Čulkov was opposing a major tenet of Russian neo-classicism as exemplified in the tragedies of Sumarokov, namely that good proceeds from reason and evil from passion. There is a deliberate jibe in the high-sounding phrase about 'reason'. Čulkov then turns back to his own case:

> Knowing this and seeing it with my own eyes every minute, do I not have just cause for hating the Muses, Apollo and the whole of Parnassus, the causes of my unhappiness? I loved them and would have loved them forever had they been a little richer, but sometimes I feel just like selling the whole of Parnassus, Muses and Apollo and all, for fifty kopeks. But the trouble is that I cannot find a single ignoramus who will give me even a kopek for them.

He is angered when he sees a vulgar and almost illiterate bureaucrat who has robbed people and married off his daughter to a wealthy general, and now drives about town in a fine carriage:

> There is an example of fate's justice; he is more immoral than I am, but rich; more stupid than I am, but composed; he deserves contempt, but he is supremely happy. Ah, fate, why did you make me a writer; it would have been better had I been an office clerk.

In this instance the concept of fate is not merely a literary device, although of course Čulkov expressed himself in this way because he was imbued with the attitudes of his time. Complaints against fate are as common in his works as they are in the works of his contemporaries, but for a man in his situation they must have frequently had more than a purely literary or intellectual appeal.

The passages quoted above may suggest that Čulkov was unemployed and in fact was attempting to make a fulltime career of writing and publishing. However, by 1772 he was in government service once again. Nikolaj Novikov in his *Attempt at an Historical Dictionary of Russian Writers* refers to Čulkov as 'a collegiate registering clerk attached to the governing Senate'. This means that Čulkov held the fourteenth and lowest rank in the Table of Ranks established by Peter the Great in 1722 for government service, both civilian and military. Evidently, he meant what he said about the sad lot of the professional writer, and had taken the appropriate action.

According to Soviet scholars, Čulkov began working at the Department of Commerce (*Kommerc-Kollegija*) in 1772. He owed his assignment to this Department to Prince Aleksandr Alekseevič Vjazemskij, the Procurator-General in Catherine's government. Čulkov mentions this fact with gratitude in dedicating to Vjazemskij his monumental history of Russian commerce which began to appear in 1781.[43] The Department of Commerce was established by order of the Tsar Peter in 1712 and during the eighteenth century it played a modest role in supervising and promoting Russian trade. Working in this Department Čulkov would of course have had access to a great deal of factual material essential for the compilation of his history of Russian commerce and a number of other works he produced in his later years.

Another, and more famous, writer also worked in the Department of Commerce during the seventies and eighties. E. V. Prikazčikova, in the collective work *The History of Russian Economic Thought*, shows that Aleksandr Radiščev, who was arrested in 1790 and later exiled to Siberia as a radical, joined the Department in 1777. It appears that documents exist demonstrating that Radiščev and Čulkov worked together on a number of official matters.[44]

The year 1772 marks a turning point in Čulkov's career, for from this point on he became increasingly concerned with the compilation of non-literary works. Consequently, his own original writing in prose and in verse was pushed aside. His history of Russian commerce seems to have occupied almost all of his time and energy during the latter part of the seventies and most of the eighties. After seeing his *Collection of Various Songs* (*Sobranie raznyx pesen*) through the press he published nothing for several years. This work contained some songs written by contemporary writers such as Sumarokov, but it is best known as the first printed collection of folk songs in Russia. It was

[43] *Istoričeskoe opisanie rossijskoj kommercii*, 7 vols. (St. Petersburg, later Moscow, 1781-1788).

[44] "Ideolog kupečestva M. D. Čulkov", in Vol. I of *Istorija russkoj èkonomičeskoj mysli*, ed. A. I. Paškov (Moscow, 1955), p. 490. This standard text is now available in English: *A History of Russian Economic Thought*, ed. J. M. Letiche (Berkeley & Los Angeles, 1964). The translation is not reliable throughout.

extremely popular during Čulkov's lifetime and circulated widely in at least four editions.

We have a letter written by Čulkov to an unknown person requesting his intercession with the Empress so that 'the remainder' of the song collection might be published. The letter is dated July 19, 1776.[45] One wonders why it was necessary for Čulkov to request that the Empress herself be petitioned regarding what seems to be a routine matter: the earlier parts of his song collection had been published already without any need for Catherine's permission. Several writers had had problems with the censorship since the end of 1769, when it was partially responsible for a number of satirical journals' ceasing publication. The outbreak of the Pugačëv Rebellion in May of 1773 made Catherine very sensitive to any manifestation of 'popular' culture and therefore it is not entirely impossible that her censors regarded some of the peasant songs in Čulkov's collection as most incendiary material and hence declined to pass them for publication. However, it may be that Čulkov was simply requesting a government subsidy to complete publication of the work.

Similarly, one can hypothesize that the Pugačëv Rebellion and the hypersensitivity to subversive ideas that it aroused in high places played some part in Čulkov's prolonged withdrawal from literary pursuits. But there is absolutely no evidence that his decision was influenced in any way by these events, any more than similar decisions to abandon literature proper made by such men as Lukin, Fonvizin, Karamzin, or Ivan Dmitriev. Once again we come back to the essential fact that it was simply not possible for a man to make a career as a professional writer, and indeed few men would have wished to even if they could: literary excellence by itself carried little merit. The point has already been made that this was still an age of court poets and aristocratic patrons. There did not as yet exist a reading public which could support an independent author. One must also remember that in eighteenth-century Russia government service, either civilian or military, offered really the only outlet for the abilities and ambitions of the talented man.[46] In these circumstances Čulkov's decision to enter government service and make it his career was entirely realistic and becomes readily understandable.

[45] *Arxiv Direkcii imp. teatrov* (St. Petersburg, 1902), Part 2, pp. 99-100. Čulkov's letter probably refers to a second edition of the collection, since the first edition appeared in four parts in 1770 to 1774.

[46] Marc Raeff, *Origins of the Russian Intelligentsia: The Eighteenth-Century Nobility* (New York, 1966).

At the beginning of this chapter I expressed regret that Čulkov does not figure in the memoirs of the Catherine period. There is, however, one quite brief and also curious mention of Čulkov in the memoirs of Aleksandr Mixajlovič Turgenev.[47] Turgenev argues that Princess Daškova was hoping to gain some glory for herself by having the Academy, of which she was then Director, publish Čulkov's work on Russian commerce. She kept a manuscript of Čulkov's, sent to her by the Empress, for three years without doing anything with it, loath to have it credited to him rather than to herself. Čulkov refused to permit this, obtained two months' leave of absence from his position at the Department of Commerce, and took his manuscript to Moscow where Nikolaj Novikov completed the printing in six weeks.[48] On his return to the capital Čulkov submitted copies of his work to the Empress, who accepted them graciously and rewarded the diligent author with a gold snuffbox decorated with diamonds. Catherine then taxed Princess Daškova with her dilatoriness and poked fun at her, making her a gift of one volume of Čulkov's work. It is Turgenev's contention that Daškova was enraged and vented her anger upon Novikov at the first opportunity by instigating the suppression of the Masons, of which Novikov was a leading light.

Turgenev's memoirs are not regarded as reliable, and this piece of court scandal raises more questions than it answers and contains a number of factual errors. For example, Čulkov's patronymic is given as 'Petrovič'. Nor does the behavior attributed to Princess Daškova appear likely from what we know of her personality. As so often with available biographical information about Čulkov, we are left with only scattered details, wondering which can be credited and which cannot. Turgenev's anecdote does suggest an explanation for the curious circumstance whereby the first volume of Čulkov's work was published by the Academy of Sciences in St. Petersburg, whereas the remainder from the second book of Volume II was printed in Moscow at the University press leased by Novikov. Possibly printing of the work was begun in St. Petersburg, but was then held up for some unknown reason. We may conclude from this episode that Čulkov's relationship with Novikov was reasonably close, since he turned to him when confronted with obstacles put in his way by the Director of the Russian

[47] "Zapiski Aleksandra Mixajloviča Turgeneva", *Russkaja starina*, Vol. 53 (1887), No. 1, 102-104.

[48] Novikov rented the printing press of Moscow University from 1779 until 1789.

Academy. But one must also remember that there were few publishing houses available to Čulkov at that time; the decree permitting private ownership of printing presses did not become effective until 1783.

For most of the eighties Čulkov was occupied with the writing of his multi-volume history of Russian commerce, finally completed in 1788. However, he did publish in 1782 a *Dictionary of Russian Superstitions* (*Slovar' russkix sueverij*), which was dedicated to 'M* S*** G***'.[49] The initials almost certainly stand for Mixail Sergeevič Golikov. Čulkov lavished praise upon this famous and enormously wealthy merchant for his many good works, including his contribution to help pay for the celebrated Falconet statue of Peter the Great in St. Petersburg. He also expressed his gratitude to Golikov for paying his son's way at the 'best university in Europe'. Čulkov does not tell us which one this might be.

Clearly, by this time Čulkov was no longer poor. He continued in his position at the Department of Commerce and dedicated each of his serious and learned works to an influential patron. We may be sure that his financial situation was now secured. If Čulkov remembered his complaints of poverty and the injustice of fate that he published late in 1769 in his journal *This and That*, it was probably with a smile of self-satisfaction. Now he could afford to ride in a rich carriage like the bureaucrat of whom he had complained earlier. As a man of very modest social background, Čulkov sought not only money but a respectable position in society. In this he succeeded. He had sufficient funds in 1783 to buy himself a small estate named Kovkino in Moscow Province.[50] He had managed to become a landowner through his hard work as a government official and through the patronage of highly placed people. Čulkov was himself an example of the 'vertical hero' so common in the novels of the eighteenth and nineteenth centuries, and

[49] *Slovar' russkix sueverij* (St. Petersburg, 1782). The munificent merchant Golikov went bankrupt in 1783.

[50] A. Fomin, "K biografii M. D. Čulkova (Rod. 1740 g-um. 1793 g.)", *Knigovedenie*, Nos. 7-8 (1894), p. 16. Fomin also quotes a document showing that Čulkov petitioned on December 3, 1789 that he be listed as a noble of Moscow Province. This suggests that he felt he had a right to be so listed, but it is not clear from Fomin's note whether Čulkov's petition was granted or not. Vsevolodskij-Gerngross, in his *Russkij teatr vtoroj poloviny XVIII veka* (Moscow, 1960), p. 112, states that Čulkov "became a member of the nobility in 1789, receiving land and serfs in the Dmitrov district near Moscow (his archive is preserved in the Dmitrov Regional Museum)." I have not been able to learn anything further about this archive.

indeed in some of his own prose fiction. However, his way was far less exciting and adventurous than that of the heroes of novels.

It was on his newly acquired estate of Kovkino that in 1785 Čulkov composed his "Instruction to My Young Son About to Enter Service".[51] Čulkov's civil service career and his acquaintance with those in authority and with influential patrons had their effect upon his personality. His "Instruction" suggests quite a different type of man from the author of the bantering, ironic and irreverent prose fiction of some fifteen years earlier. It is divided into eleven numbered sections, consisting usually of one paragraph each. Čulkov urges his son to honor God, the Empress and the Imperial family, and to feel respect for 'distinguished personages' (*znatnye osoby*). Furthermore, his son should keep quiet about the weaknesses of his superiors and not discuss secret matters with anyone, not even relatives or friends. He should hold his credit sacred and not seek high office or wealth. Čulkov then recommends seven works for his son's edification, none of which was written by a Russian. They are as follows: Rousseau, *Discours sur les sciences et les arts*; Pope, *Essay on Man*; *Socrates, Moral Sayings*(?); Epictetus, *Enchiridion* and *Apophthegmata*; Cebes, *Picture of the World* [known in Latin as *Cebetis Tabula*]; Bitaubé, the poem *Joseph*; and Marmontel, *Bélisaire*.[52] "But", warns Čulkov, "you must study and learn most of all the Holy Scripture, the laws of the land, and know our own vast country and other states." And he concludes his advice: "The whole purpose and intent of this testament is to assure that you will be pleasing unto God in your actions, useful to the sovereign, necessary to society and a worthy inheritor of your father's estate, which he acquired through unremitting labor."

In the recommendations that he makes to his son on what to read and how to behave Čulkov does of course reveal a considerable amount of information about himself and the road he had taken in order to achieve what he considered to be an honored and respectable position

[51] "Nastavlenie maloletnomu synu moemu vstupajuščemu v službu", in *Ekonomičeskie zapiski* (Moscow, 1788). Čulkov explains that it was written on May 9, 1785; he had decided to publish it because so many people were making unauthorized and inaccurate copies of it.

[52] This list is of course in Russian and it is hard sometimes to discover exactly which author or work is meant. The Russian is as follows (in the accusative case): "Russo, Rassuždenija o čeloveke; Poppija, Opyt o čeloveke; Sokrata, Nravoučenie; Epikteta, Enxiridion i apoftegmy; Kevita, Kartinu sveta; Bitobe, poèmu Iosifa; Marmontelja, Velizarija". The Socrates item might well refer to the work of Jacob Vernet translated into Russian as *Sokratičeskie razgovory* (St. Petersburg, 1777). An earlier translation appeared in 1769.

in Russian society. The rather grave and earnest reading material he commends to his son's attention is equally 'respectable'. It could well be that the widely read Radiščev had drawn Čulkov's attention to some of these works. Čulkov never displays any interest in works of this sort in the sixties and early seventies.

A second edition of the four parts of *The Mocker* appeared in Moscow in 1783 and 1784, and a third edition in 1789, with a fifth part added.[53] It seems reasonable to conclude that this fifth part was written some time between 1784 and 1789. Čulkov managed to maintain the general tone of the tales, but some of the additional stories are more pointed in their social satire and have a more serious and solemn nature that obviously reflects the change in his own personality. During this period Čulkov continued to display his interest in less literary matters. Presumably in order to make available to a wider public the results of his extensive reading and research, he abstracted certain sections of his much larger work on Russian commerce. Hence we find him publishing such shorter volumes as his *Brief History of Russian Trade* and *Essential Instructions for Russian Merchants*.[54]

Right to the end of his life Čulkov did not cease to extend the range of his interests. He published a book of cures for common diseases that afflict both human beings and animals, and also worked on a large compilation of Russian laws, publication of which was not completed until after his death.[55] In his autobiographical note of 1790 Čulkov had listed this latter work among nine unpublished items. The only other work that has come down to us is his comedy "Call It What You Will" which survived in an actor's copy of 1783. The remainder apparently consisted of some commercial works, and one item with the intriguing title: "Project for a Treaty between European Sovereigns for the Eternal Abolition of War in Europe" – Čulkov was evidently prepared

[53] *Peresmešnik, ili Slavenskie skazki*, 3rd ed. rev., 5 parts in 3 vols. (Moscow, 1789). The Library of Congress has a copy of this rare work. Cambridge University Library possesses the second edition (1783-1784), bound with the fifth part of the third edition (1789). In his *Čulkov i Levšin* (pp. 42, 77) Šklovskij contends that a second edition appeared in 1770, but this does not figure in any of the bibliographies: this is almost certainly a *tisnenie* or reprint, not a separate edition.

[54] *Istorija (kratkaja) rossijskoj torgovli* (Moscow, 1788); and *Nastavlenie neobxodimo nužnoe dlja rossijskix kupcov* (Moscow, 1791).

[55] *Lečebnik sel'skij*, 5 parts (Moscow, 1789-1790); and *Slovar' juridičeskij*, 2 vols. (Moscow 1792-1796). The card in the catalogue of the Lenin Library in Moscow states that this latter work was completed by an unknown hand after Čulkov's death. Čulkov's name is given only on the title pages of the first part and of the first section of the second part.

to turn his hand to any problem, however intimidating. One work which might have been of special interest to the literary historian has the title: "The Pretender Griška Otrep'ev, a satirical poem in nine cantos".[56]

The picture we get of him from his "Instruction" to his son is that of a model subject and devoted civil servant. There is no evidence that Čulkov was ever a Mason, although as Boris Tomaševskij has pointed out, his list of seven recommended books includes two, those by Epictetus and Cebes of Thebes, that enjoyed popularity in Russian Masonic circles.[57] Late in 1791, that is more than a year after Radiščev had been imprisoned, Catherine displayed her confidence in Čulkov's ability and loyalty when she decided to add him to a special group of advisors and commented on his 'efficiency and promptness'.[58]

It would not be unfair to portray Čulkov as a man who tried a number of occupations, including that of professional writer, in an attempt to become wealthy and respectable. In this he was a typical representative of the bourgeois mentality. In many ways his life may be considered a success story. Overcoming the disadvantage of obscure origins, he had managed to get some education, then made contacts with the literary world of the time through his association with the Russian court theater in St. Petersburg and his numerous works in verse and prose. Later his learned compilations brought him to the attention of influential patrons and high government officials. When Čulkov found that success in the literary world brought little tangible reward, he sought to make his way in government service. Novikov refers to him in 1772 as a collegiate registering clerk, but Čulkov himself tells us in 1790 that he is a court councillor (*nadvornyj sovetnik*). Thus in the space of eighteen years he had risen from the fourteenth or lowest rank in the civil service to the seventh. His rise in government service was hardly meteoric, but an achievement nonetheless. By the end of his life Čulkov had acquired a small estate and so become a member of the landowning gentry, as well as a trusted official who enjoyed the confidence of the Empress. What we might call his pursuit of gentility ended happily.

[56] This must have been written in the early part of his career, because it is included in a list of his works inside the back cover of Part IV of his *Sobranie raznyx pesen* (St. Petersburg, 1774). Otrep'ev was of course the "false Dimitrij."
[57] *Iroi-komičeskaja poèma*, p. 192.
[58] Catherine's letter of November 1, 1791 to Nikolaj Petrovič Arxarov is quoted in *Iroi-komičeskaja poèma*, p. 193.

II

ROMANCE AND ANTI-ROMANCE IN *THE MOCKER*

An important point to bear in mind is the very fact of Čulkov's modest background, of his non-noble origin. Whether he was the son of a merchant or of a priest, he clearly had the opportunity to hear and read the manuscript tales that were so popular among the lower and middle classes in the seventeenth and early eighteenth centuries, and indeed much later. At the same time, his education in the Gymnasium of Moscow University and later cultural environment introduced him to a 'higher' literary tradition, that of neo-classicism in its special Russian garb. Čulkov soon learned French, and some elements of Western European literature became known to him at first hand. Consequently, he was at home in three separate cultural areas, and not entirely a captive of any special part of his cultural background. This multiplicity of influences affects his work, most particularly his prose fiction, and lends to it features which distinguish it from that produced by his contemporaries.

Čulkov's claims to the interest of literary historians are many and varied, but rest mainly upon his two major works of prose fiction *The Mocker, or Slavic Tales* and a short, incomplete novel *The Comely Cook, or the Adventures of a Depraved Woman.*[1] The vital role played by Čulkov in the rise of a narrative prose tradition and specifically of the indigenous Russian novel has long been acknowledged. He was an innovator, and moreover at a time when the most influential writers

[1] *Prigožaja povarixa, ili poxoždenie razvratnoj ženščiny*, I (St. Petersburg, 1770). A third prose work is not available in the United States and possibly not outside the Soviet Union: *Poxoždenie Axillesovo pod imjamen Pirry do Trojanskija osady* (St. Petersburg, 1769); a second edition appeared in Moscow in 1788. There is an outline of the plot in V. V. Sipovskij, *Očerki po istorii russkogo romana*, I (St. Petersburg, 1909), pp. 449-450. The work is modeled along the lines of the ancient Greek romance or French heroic novel and recounts an adventure of Achilles before the Trojan War. As in part of the later legend, Achilles is shown disguised as a girl; Čulkov supplies the name Pyrrha, a girl's name which occurs in Latin, e.g., Horace.

who held sway for the greater part of the century, placed verse genres at the top of their hierarchy of literary values, relegating prose to a very modest position except when it was used in lofty rhetoric. This hierarchy of literary values was modeled on the theories of Boileau in France and his chief Russian disciple Sumarokov. Both Sumarokov and his older rival Lomonosov held prose fiction in very low esteem and were particularly offended by the type of fiction that was beginning to enter Russia from France in the middle of the century: for example, *Gil Blas* by Le Sage. In his *Rhetoric*, published in 1748, Lomonosov spoke harshly of French tales "which are called novels (*romany*)".[2] He compared such novels to manuscript tales like "Prince Bova" ("Bova Korolevič") and condemned them as foolish and without moral value. A dozen years later Sumarokov published his often-qouted attack on novels in his journal *The Industrious Bee*. In much the same terms as Lomonosov, he complained that reading such works was a complete waste of a thinking man's time.[3]

The novel genre did, however, have its defenders at this time, and in particular among the teachers and students of the Cadet School (*Suxoputnyj šljaxetnyj kadeckij korpus*), where several novels were translated and also printed. A spirited defense of novels was included by the anonymous translator in his Foreword to Prévost's *Le philosophe anglois, ou Histoire de monsieur Cleveland, fils naturel de Cromwell,* which was published at the Cadet School press in 1760.[4] In this Foreword, which is almost certainly a response to Sumarokov's attack of the previous year, the translator fights the opponents of novels on their own terms; he insists on the moral purpose and usefulness of the novel genre. Taking note of recent attacks on the genre, he suggests that a

[2] Mixail Lomonosov, *Kratkoe rukovodstvo k krasnorečiju (Razdelenie pervoe, sostojaščee iz Ritoriki)*, in *Sočinenija* (Moscow, 1957), p. 326. Lomonosov excluded from general condemnation Fénelon's *Les aventures de Télémaque* and John Barclay's *Argenis*; the moralizing tone of both works is very pronounced, so much so that they cease to be novels at all.

[3] Aleksandr Sumarokov, "O čtenii romanov", *Trudoljubivaja pčela* (St. Petersburg, 1759), p. 374) Sumarokov also makes an exception of *Télémaque* and praises *Don Quixote*. The discussion as to the value or malevolent influence of novels did of course go on for several decades well into the nineteenth century. See, for example: N. Belozerskaja, "Vlijanie perevodnogo romana i zapadnoj civilizacii na russkoe obščestvo XVIII veka", *Russkaja starina*, Vol. 83 (January 1895), 151-153.

[4] *Filozof Aglinskoj, ili žitiё Klevelanda, pobočnogo syna Kromveleva, samim im pisannoe*, I (St. Petersburg, 1760). I. Z. Serman states in the collaborative volume *Istorija russkogo romana*, I (Moscow-Leningrad, 1962), p. 50, that the author of this Foreword was S. A. Porošin, who also translated Prévost's novel. There is a copy of this edition in the Library of Congress.

number of bad novels that had of late appeared in France and Germany were to blame and remarks: "We are not alone in having such works as 'Prince Bova', 'Eruslan Lazarevič', and 'Peter of the Golden Keys'. You find many of them everywhere." The translator obviously intended to underline the difference between such tales and modern novels. He goes on to argue that there are good and bad novels, just as there were good and bad authors in Classical Antiquity and in seventeenth-century France (note the authorities). He ends with a plea for fairness: "Novels can also be useful. It seems to me, therefore, that impartiality should prevent people from thundering against them so unmercifully." This last comment undoubtedly refers to Sumarokov, who was notoriously opinionated and bad-tempered.

The disagreement was in part the result of woolly terminology. Russian writers of the eighteenth century, so conscious of the distinction of genre in verse, were very casual in their attitude towards genre in prose fiction, chiefly because no major figure had come forward and attempted the sort of codification of prose genres, provided for example by Huet and others in seventeenth-century France.[5] The problem was further aggravated in the case of the novel since the Russians borrowed the French word *roman*, which could be used for both 'novel' and 'romance'. In their condemnation of what they called *romany* both Lomonosov and Sumarokov seem to have lumped romances and novels together. They had no concept of the development of prose fiction from one type or style to another.[6]

[5] For the considerable discussion of the genre in France at that period see Moses Ratner, *Theory and Criticism of the Novel in France from* L'Astrée *to 1750* (New York, 1938).

[6] On this problem of terminology see: V. Kožinov, *Proisxoždenie romana: teoretiko-istoričeskij očerk* (Moscow, 1963), pp. 58ff. For a detailed account of the way such terms as *roman, skazka*, and *povest'* were used in Russia during the eighteenth century, see: Peter Brang, *Studien zu Theorie und Praxis der russischen Erzählung 1770-1811* (Wiesbaden, 1960), pp. 36-52. In the Preface to his story *Incognita* (1692), Congreve includes the following delightful description of romances and novels: "Romances are generally composed of the Constant Loves and invincible Courages of Hero's, Heroins, Kings and Queens, Mortals of the first Rank, and so forth; where lofty Language, miraculous Contingencies and impossible Performances, elevate and surprize the Reader into a giddy Delight, which leaves him flat upon the Ground whenever he gives of[f], and vexes him to think how he had suffer'd himself to be pleased and transported, concern'd and afflicted at the Several Passages which he has Read, viz. these Knights Success to their Damosels Misfortunes, and such like, when he is forced to be very well convinced that 'tis all a lye. Novels are of a more familiar Nature; Come near us, and represent to us Intrigues in practice, delight us with Accidents and odd events, but not such as are wholly unusual or unpresidented, such which not being so distant

The defense of novels to which we have referred, and also the fact that they continued to be translated in spite of the oracular pronouncements of men like Sumarokov, shows that Čulkov was not operating entirely in a vacuum. However, the defense was predicated on the neo-classical view of literature's moral purpose. Furthermore, the translating of novels is still not the same thing as the producing of original prose fiction, which was one of Čulkov's chief contributions to Russian literary history.

Čulkov did not produce the first printed novel in Russia; that honor belongs to Fëdor Èmin, whose novel *Inconstant Fortune, or the Adventures of Miramond* appeared in 1763.[7] Èmin deliberately shrouded his origins in mystery, but it seems that he was born in the Ukraine and traveled widely in the Ottoman Empire and in Europe, getting as far as London before returning to Russia in 1761. He professed to put something of his own adventures into his lengthy novels, but they in fact lean heavily on the French novels of adventure or romances of the seventeenth century. The eighteenth century was, after all, a time when Russians were attempting to regain their rightful place in the cultural life of Europe and it is no surprise that they should have had to undergo a period of apprenticeship before making valid contributions of their own. The novel genre, and indeed prose fiction in general, was almost completely unknown in Russian printed literature until the middle of the century, but then suddenly achieved enormous popularity with the as yet small Russian reading public. By recent count over a thousand novels were published during the reign of Catherine II. However, by far the great majority of the most widely read novels at that period were translations of foreign works, mostly French. What is more, as in the case of Èmin's works, those Russian novels that did meet with a favorable response were usually heavily indebted to foreign models. As late as 1791 that voracious novel reader Andrej Bolotov remarked with evident regret that there were all too few novels that could be called truly Russian.[8]

---

from our Belief bring also the pleasure nearer us. Romances give more of Wonder, Novels more Delight." Quoted in L. G. Scaliger, "*Don Quixote* as a Prose Epic", *Forum for Modern Language Studies*, II (Edinburgh, 1966), No. 1, 54-55. As Scaliger adds, "in this passage one can see the modern English sense of the term [novel] struggling to be born".

[7] *Nepostojannaja Fortuna, ili poxoždenie Miramonda* (St. Petersburg, 1763). The hero travels over a large part of the world on his extraordinary adventures.

[8] "Mysli i bespristrastnye suždenija o romanax, kak original'nyx rossijskix, tak i perevedënnyx s inostrannyx jazykov Andreja Bolotova", *Literaturnoe nesledstvo,*

Prose fiction had however been popular in Russia for several decades, well before the appearance of the first printed novel, in the form of the so-called manuscript tales. These tales, which circulated widely in cheap hand-written copies very much like the English chapbooks, ranged from the picaresque and satirical to the idealistic romance. They belonged to a popular sub-literature flourishing beneath the high, neo-classical literature, much of it in verse, which appeared in expensive books. In this respect the situation in Russia was broadly similar to that of seventeenth-century France. As Antoine Adam has remarked: "C'est que nous ne comprenons guère cette époque si nous n'avons pas dans l'esprit l'existence, à travers tout le siècle, de deux littératures juxtaposées, ou plus exactement, superposées. Au-dessus, celle des doctes et de l'Académie, la seule que daigne discuter la critique, la 'belle littérature', comme l'on dit alors, c'est-à-dire, en fait, celle qui se conforme aux enseignements de l'humanisme et qui s'inspire des modèles de l'Antiquité. Au-dessous, celle que les doctes dédaignent ou lisent en cachette; que la critique ignore et qui ignore la critique; celle qui va chercher ses sujets et ses modeles dans les oeuvres romanesques des siècles précédents." [9]

We have already seen that because of his social background, Čulkov would have known many, if not most, of the manuscript tales then in circulation. Indeed, references to them do occur in his works. Thus, for example, in his journal *This and That* (Week 10) he tells of a retired clerk who managed to earn his keep by making copies of such tales, the best known of which are "Prince Bova" ("Bova Korolevič"), "Peter of the Golden Keys" ("Pëtr zlatyx ključej"), "Eruslan Lazarevič", "The Russian Nobleman Alexander" ("Rossijskij dvorjanin Aleksandr"), and "Frol Skobeev". Čulkov ends his list with the apparently sarcastic phrase: "and other extremely edifying stories". This tone of condescension is perfectly understandable in a young man who had received a formal (though incomplete) education at the Moscow University Gymnasium, where rhetoric and Latin literature were taught and held up as models. At the same time Čulkov came to these tales before reading neo-classical literature and theorists and he never quite embraced the didactic theories urged by Sumarokov and Lomonosov.

Nos. 9-10 (1933), p. 214. Bolotov makes his comment in a review of *Rossijskaja Pamela* (1789) by Pavel L'vov.

[9] See Adam's introduction to the Pléiade edition *Romanciers du XVII-e siècle* (Paris, 1958).

If he had, he would probably not have written prose fiction at all, or certainly not the type he did.

The tales consisted for the most part of borrowings from Western Europe. "Prince Bova" was a migratory tale that originated in France in the thirteenth century but did not reach Russia until the sixteenth century by way of Belorussia. "Peter of the Golden Keys" was also a medieval French romance and was translated into Russian from a Polish text in 1680. "Eruslan Lazarevič" entered Russia in the sixteenth century but by a somewhat different route: it tells episodes from the tenth-century Persian epic *Shahname* by Firdausi and passed into Russia via the Cossacks following their contacts with the Crimean Tartars.

However, tales like "Frol Skobeev", "The Russian Nobleman Alexander", and also "The Russian Sailor Vasilij Koriockij" ("Rossijskij matros Vasilij Koriockij"), which Čulkov omits from his list, belong to a second and more recent native tradition of prose fiction in Russia.[10] They were written in Russia during and immediately after the Petrine period. Frol Skobeev (*circa* 1700) presents a striking contrast to the heroes in the tales of chivalry, for he is a rogue and slanderer, very reminiscent of the *picaro*. The tale about Alexander recalls the French seventeenth-century novels of adventure, but it lacks their heroic idealism. The hero Alexander dies and his place in the narrative is taken by a friend Vladimir, who often approaches Frol Skobeev in his outlook on life and especially on women. One notes also that both Alexander and Vasilij Koriockij are Russians who go abroad to Europe to seek fame and fortune. Frol stays home but he too is primarily interested in achieving success, socially and financially.

The important point to be remembered is that the tales presented two broad traditions of narrative prose. The first, and by far the older, tradition was that of the tale of chivalry or heroic romance, and it was this type of tale that dominated in Russia in the seventeenth and early eighteenth centuries. But there was a second type of tale, satirical in tone and partially designed as an anti-romance. "Frol Skobeev" is a good example of this type of tale, and we shall see a little later that one of the longer stories in *The Mocker*, involving the adventures of an impecunious but wily young student, has a number of features in common with it.

[10] These two tales, together with a third "Povest' o šljaxeckom syne", are reproduced with textual variants and a full commentary by G. N. Moiseeva in her book *Russkie povesti pervoj treti XVIII veka* (Moscow-Leningrad, 1965).

Such, then, were the two 'native' traditions of narrative prose fiction upon which Čulkov was able to draw. I have already quoted the apparently sarcastic comment with which Čulkov closed his list of popular manuscript tales in his journal *This and That*. Whether or not this comment is an indication of his own considered opinion of them is hard to say. What is obvious is that he did read these tales and was undoubtedly influenced by their themes. In fact, a few direct echoes of the tales do occur in his prose. These generally involve the borrowing of episodes, although Čulkov seems to have been amused by the notion of reworking "Prince Bova" into an epic poem in verse. He satirizes such a plan in the grotesque figure of the old dwarf Kuromša in *The Mocker*, who has spent thirty years at this task.[11] An example of Čulkov's borrowing from the tales occurs in *The Mocker* when a centaur-like creature named Polkan appears and is defeated in single combat by the hero Siloslav. This episode is obviously borrowed from "Prince Bova".[12] A further direct borrowing from another of the tales we have mentioned – "Eruslan Lazarevič" – occurs elsewhere in *The Mocker*. This is the bizarre episode of the severed head that the hero Siloslav comes across on a battlefield strewn with corpses and weapons. Siloslav waits patiently until the head has recounted its sad story, then helps it regain its body, wife and throne.[13]

It is illustrative of the cultural time lag between Western Europe and Russia that there are strong echoes of French seventeenth-century literature in the prose traditions in Russia upon which Čulkov was able to draw. Since the majority of the manuscript tales owed a considerable debt to foreign models (when they were not simply translations), it is not surprising that when Čulkov turned to Western European literature, and more precisely to French literature, for inspiration and nourish-

[11] *Peresmešnik, ili Slavenskie skazki*, Part IV (Moscow, 1789), p. 182. I have used the third edition which is available in the Rare Book Division of the Library of Congress. A satirical reference to a man with similar aim occurs in Čulkov's poem "Stixi na kačeli" ("Verses on a Ferris wheel"), *I to i së* (Weeks 16-18).

[12] *Peresmešnik*, Part II, pp. 58 and 65. In "Prince Bova" Polkan knocks Bova off his horse, but is then defeated by the horse. Bova and Polkan become allies. However, soon after, the unfortunate Polkan is attacked and devoured by lions. Further on the creature Polkan see B. O. Unbegaun, "Polkan, oder vom italienischen Halbhund zum russischen Kriegsschiff", *Zeitschrift für slavische Philologie*, XVIII (1960), 58-72.

[13] *Peresmešnik*, Part I, p. 121. In "Eruslan Lazarevič" the head helps the hero to overcome his foe the Green King by teaching him how to deceive with flattery, and also gives him a special sword concealed beneath itself. Readers of Puškin's narrative poem *Ruslan i Ljudmila* (1820) will recall that it too contains an episode with a giant head on a battlefield.

ment, he found the same two broad traditions of narrative fiction and in roughly the same proportions. Following the categories suggested by George Saintsbury, we may say that in the first half of the seventeenth century French prose fiction flowed in four main streams.[14] The first was the Pastoral, represented by the *Astrée* of Honoré d'Urfé; the second was the heroic novel, whose most famous representative was the vast *Artamène ou le Grand Cyrus* by Madeleine de Scudéry; the third was the fairy tale, practiced by Madame d'Aulnoy and Perrault; and the fourth was the comic, the burlesque, or anti-romance, the best-known example of which was the *Roman comique* by Paul Scarron. The first three categories tend to form a recognizable group as far as subject matter and narrative treatment are concerned, while the fourth stands alone and in an obvious reaction against them.

An important addition to the first group, and more particularly to the third category, was Antoine Galland's translation of the Arabian Nights (*Milles et une nuits*), which appeared in twelve volumes from 1704 to 1717.[15] It seems very likely that this work was an important factor in Čulkov's decision to produce his own collection of tales. His contemporaries could not have failed to notice the similarities between the two works, and indeed the anonymous author of the "Nachricht von einigen russischen Schriftstellern" remarked of Čulkov in 1768 that "Man hat auch slavonische Fabeln von ihm, ein Werk, das in dem Geschmack der Tausend und einen Nacht, wenn gleich nicht ganz so gut, ist." *The Mocker* consists of a series of tales related by two young men. The first is Ladon, who has a flair for telling stories, and the second is a renegade monk (never named), who had been obliged to enter a monastery after getting into mischief with a landowner's wife.

Such collections of tales are of course perfectly familiar in most European literatures. The most famous examples of the successful frame story are provided by Chaucer and Boccaccio. In both the *Canterbury Tales* and the *Decameron* there are several narrators and the tales range from pious to ribald. Boccaccio included both romantic *novelle* and anti-romantic *novelle* in his work, and he was in fact the

[14] George Saintsbury, *A History of the French Novel*, I (London, 1917), p. 234. I have also found very useful *A Critical Bibliography of French Literature*, Gen. Eds. David C. Cabeen and Jules Brody. Vol. III: *The Seventeenth Century* (Syracuse University Press, 1961). See the third chapter on "Fictional Prose" in which Honoré d'Urfé and Madeleine de Scudéry are listed under "Précieux Novel" and Gomberville and La Calprenède under "Heroic Novel".

[15] The first parts of a Russian translation of Galland's version began to appear in 1763, just prior to the appearance of Čulkov's *Peresmešnik*.

initiator of the anti-romantic tale, which found its best-known successor in the *Cent nouvelles nouvelles* of the mid-fifteenth century. It should therefore be clear that collections of tales in prose are a part of an old European tradition and that they appear as a prelude to the novel genre. In producing such a collection Čulkov was not displaying any originality, but he may justly claim to have taken the first step towards the establishment of a native tradition in printed prose fiction, and in particular of the novel genre in Russia.

Unlike Chaucer and Boccaccio, Čulkov has only two narrators in the main part of his work, although in the frame story some other characters do tell short tales of their own. Čulkov's two narrators may be seen as telling romantic and anti-romantic *novelle*, to use terms familiar in other literatures. The frame story is told in the first person by Ladon, a young man who has found a place for himself in the provincial household of a retired colonel and his wife because of his talent for telling stories.[16] Ladon tells us that he is possibly illegitimate; his father was a Jew, his mother a gypsy who died bringing him into the world. Ladon's parents are obviously selected by the author for their unacceptability, not so much in contemporary Russian society as in the romances of the time, the heroes and heroines of which were always nobly born and of course never illegitimate.[17]

We are introduced to some of the colonel's unsavory neighbors and to some of his parasitic house guests, a number of whom tell interpolated tales of their own.[18] The chief plot line of the frame story is provided by the young monk, who pretends to be a ghost in order to scare everyone away while he has an amorous nightly rendezvous with the colonel's housekeeper, Sivilla (that is, Sibyl). Ladon is not so easily frightened, however, and soon manages to trap the lovers in a huge trunk. The following morning Ladon brings the colonel to see the 'ghost' and his paramour. At this moment the colonel's wife is found to have died; she had fallen over and struck her head after a gargantuan banquet. Ladon tells us that the colonel was unsteady on his feet through grief and vodka. His narrative is ironical throughout. He sati-

[16] The frame story, as well as some of the short tales narrated by the young monk, are available in Vol. I of *Russkaja proza XVIII veka*, eds. A. V. Zapadov and G. P. Makogonenko (Moscow-Leningrad, 1950), pp. 89-156.

[17] Obviously this opening is part of the "rogue", anti-romance tradition which goes back in European literature to the anonymous Spanish work of the mid-sixteenth century: *La vida de Lazarillo de Tormes*.

[18] The interpolated tale is a major feature of those parts of *The Mocker* narrated by Ladon. This was also one of the main characteristics of the ancient Greek novel and the romances or novels of seventeenth-century France.

rizes the parasitic guests and neighbors who vie with one another in weeping and wailing in order to get an invitation from the colonel to the funeral feast. The young monk then proceeds to tell his own story – a brief picaresque account of his various adventures. At one point he had been captured by a band of robbers and taken to their hideout in the forest. He was entertained graciously by the robbers' chief and finally permitted to depart.[19]

The colonel generously forgives both the monk and Sivilla after listening to the story of his adventures. The monk stays on at the house and he and Ladon become close friends. A little later the bereaved colonel himself dies, leaving his young daughter Alenona quite disconsolate. In order to chase away her gloomy thoughts, the two young men gallantly offer to tell her stories. It is agreed that each evening Ladon is to tell stories about 'our ancient knights and warriors', while the young monk promises to follow each of Ladon's tales with an amusing anecdote. There then begins a series of 'evenings' after the manner of *A Thousand and One Nights*.

The proposed framework of alternating tales is by no means followed, and the young monk has a hard time getting a hearing in the five volumes of the tales which Čulkov completed. Of the one hundred evenings (or chapters consisting of between ten and twelve pages each) Ladon narrates a total of seventy, and the monk does not make an appearance after the frame story until the middle of the second volume.[20] Ladon's narrative, which is not made up of separate tales but is in fact one enormously long story that is never completed, belongs to the ancient tradition that begins with the Greek novels and continues with the medieval romance of chivalry, *Amadís de Gaula*, and culminates in the French heroic novels and novels of adventure (*romans d'aventures*) in the seventeenth century. Few of the French novels had yet appeared in Russian, but Čulkov read French and it seems reasonable to suppose that he was familiar with some of them since they were so widely known at the time. In the frame story there is a reference to 'Russian Céladons'.[21] Céladon was the hero of the *Astrée*, which had not been

[19] This episode is reminiscent of one at the very beginning of Le Sage's novel *Gil Blas*. In Book I, Chapter III of the novel the young and very naive hero is captured by robbers and taken to their lavishly appointed underground cave. Captain Rolando does not treat Gil Blas with quite the same generosity as the robber chief does the monk: Gil Blas escapes while the robbers are away. A Russian translation of *Gil Blas* first appeared in 1754-1755.

[20] Ladon narrates evenings 1 to 25, 31 to 45, 56-70, and 81 to 95 (all numbers inclusive).

[21] *Russkaja proza XVIII veka*, p. 102.

translated into Russian. One notes also the similarity between this name and that of Čulkov's hero Ladon.

The French heroic novels were set for the most part in the ancient world of Greece and Rome and were semi- or pseudo-historical. However, the *Astrée* and also the incomplete *Faramond* by La Calprenède were attempts to portray what George Sainstbury called 'misty Merovingian times'.[22] Ladon's narrative has as little to do with history as the novels of La Calprenède, and yet we can perhaps see where Čulkov obtained the idea for setting his tales in what we might call 'misty Varangian times'. In Ladon's narrative the characters are exclusively people of noble birth. The chief hero is Siloslav, prince of Vineta, a city we are told existed in 'ancient times' on the spot where St. Petersburg was built.[23] Siloslav's father is Nravoblag, one of the ideal rulers so beloved of eighteenth-century writers who composed utopias. Nravoblag, whose beneficent reign is briefly described, had been the leader of the Slavs and fought successful wars against both Rome and Greece. The chronology of Čulkov's ancient Slavic tales is, to say the least, rather unsteady: we find a blend of pagan Slavs and pagan Greeks, who live in Byzantine times, with references to Novgorod and Russian monasteries. The important point to be noted here is that Čulkov was attempting to link the ancient history of his own country with that of Greece and Rome; that is, trying to put his country 'on the map'. Čulkov, like many of his fellow countrymen, was conscious of the cultural backwardness of Russia and of the embarrassing fact that it had come late to European civilization. There is undeniably an element of cultural nationalism in Čulkov's attempt to create a respectable history for the Eastern Slavs, as in his constant substitution of Slavic pagan deities for those of Classical antiquity, obviously seeking to create a native system of mythological symbolic references.[24] In this he certainly succeeded, for many of his Slavic deities were used by later Russian writers in the eighteenth century and even in the early part of the nineteenth century. One of the important sources of Čulkov's Slavic mythological system was the *Sinopsis* of Innokentij Gizel', which was first

[22] *A History of the French Novel*, I, 234.

[23] Čulkov displayed considerable ingenuity in creating names from Russian roots, such as Siloslav ("strong Slav"), or Nravoblag ("of noble manners"). The first Russian writer to introduce such names consciously was Vladimir Lukin, who objected to the foreign names employed by Sumarokov in his tragedies.

[24] For the rise of Russian cultural nationalism see: Hans Rogger, *The Development of Russian National Consciousness in the Eighteenth Century* (Cambridge, Mass., 1960).

printed in 1674 at the Kievan Cave Monastery. This was an extremely popular book and went through several editions in the eighteenth century.[25] It served as the standard history of Kievan Russia for many years. Some of the deities that Čulkov took over from the *Sinopsis* were genuine Slavic pagan gods, for example Perun. However, some were not, for example Lada, supposedly the goddess of love. It seems that this name results from an attempt in Poland to explain a common refrain in folk songs as a variant of the Greek Leda.[26] Čulkov also did not hesitate to invent some deities of his own, for example 'Zimcerla' whom he claims as a Slavic equivalent of Aurora.

Prince Siloslav, ignoring all warnings of danger and the pleas of his father's loyal subjects, departs from Vineta in search of his beloved Prelepa ('most fair'), who has been abducted by evil spirits to a city surrounded by a huge, fearsome serpent.[27] Soberly the narrator comments that this action on the part of Siloslav shows "how much power love has over our hearts".[28] If the plot sounds familiar, it should. It is of course that of countless fairy tales, of tales in *A Thousand and One Nights*, of chivalric romances, and also incidentally of the later narrative poem *Ruslan and Ljudmila* by Puškin. Siloslav sets out on his adventures with his trusty servant Krepostan ('strong build'). They rescue a sorceress named Prevrata (from the Russian verb 'to transform'), who then in gratitude comes to Siloslav's aid somewhat later when he gets into trouble with some evil spirits. For the most part the narrative is full of impossible adventures, interlarded with visits to magical abodes, encounters with awesome monsters, and with sleeping beauties, who very frequently turn out to nourish feelings of hostility for the unsuspecting hero.

If anything, the fantastic elements increase as Ladon's narrative proceeds, and in the fifth volume one hero, Kidal, pays a visit to the moon on the back of a giant bird, albeit in a dream: this may be the first piece of space fiction in Russian literature.[29] Throughout the nar-

[25] The *Sinopsis* was one of the works Novikov mentioned in his journal *Živopisec* as being popular among urban classes in Russia who knew no foreign languages. See "N. I. Novikov" in *Sočinenija N. S. Tixonravova*, III, Part 1 (Moscow, 1898), 144.

[26] See the article "Lada" by Vsevolod Miller in the Brockhaus-Èfron encyclopedia.

[27] The name "Vineta" may have been related in Čulkov's mind to the name of one of the early Slavic tribes: "Venetae" or "Venedae". Cf. German "Wenden".

[28] *Peresmešnik*, I, 118.

[29] Such cosmic voyages were by no means unknown in French seventeenth-

rative there are frequent and prolonged descriptions of formal gardens, magnificent palaces, Classical statuary and fountains, which read like imaginative portrayals of the great palaces and formal gardens that Čulkov could well have seen in and around St. Petersburg. But the real scenes of building and gardens served only as a starting point for Čulkov: his descriptions of the places visited by his heroes are enveloped in a luxurious, Oriental splendor, which readily recalls *A Thousand and One Nights*. And in the descriptions of the formal gardens, an idealized form of the natural world prevails. Very much in the neo-classical manner, the action takes place in Arcadian groves or on delectable river banks. The climate seems to be a southern one; winter is never mentioned and there is no connection between the setting of the tales and of northern Russia. The frequent appearance of lightly clad damsels and the sumptuous surroundings have a langorous quality which is much more suggestive of the 'mysterious East'.

These elaborate descriptions are of course a common feature in the ancient Greek novels and the French heroic novels. We find many other features common to these earlier works and Ladon's narrative: the pure and almost platonic love of chivalrous hero and long-suffering heroine, the melodramatic villains, the apparent deaths, the interpolated tales, the disguises, cases of mistaken identity, and shipwrecks. We should remember that the fictional audience for these tales is a young girl Alenona, who would have preferred romances full of noble and true love, magic, strange adventures, shipwrecks, and the like. It is with considerable reluctance and only after twenty of the 'evenings' that Alenona agrees to permit the young monk to tell his first story. She would also have been pleased at the paramount importance attributed to love in Ladon's narrative, where love is itself the highest duty and there is no real concept of a possible clash between the emotional desires of the heroes and their sense of duty or responsibility. In French neo-classical drama and in the tragedies of Sumarokov, on the other hand, the action revolves around the conflict between the heroes' love and their sense of duty: in essence, the conflict is between passion which is evil and reason which is good.

Because no parts of Ladon's narrative have ever been reprinted since the third edition of *The Mocker* appeared in 1789, it may be advisable to sketch its contents at least in broad outline so as to suggest

---

century literature. See, for example: Beverly S. Ridgely, "The Cosmic Voyage in Sorel's *Francion*", *Modern Philology*, 65 (1967), No. 1, 1-8.

something of its flavor and illustrate the sizable debt Čulkov owes to the tradition of the idealistic romance or novel of chivalry.

In those parts of Ladon's narrative in which Siloslav appears, the chief mode is that of the heroic novel or novel of adventure, where love is not treated in much detail: it is taken for granted. It is in the first interpolated tale, that of Slavuron who crosses Siloslav's path, that we find love coming more into the foreground. Slavuron tells Siloslav that in his youth he had been sent to study in Constantinople, where he fell in love with Filomena, a young lady from one of the first families of the city.[30] After undergoing numerous ordeals, including a death sentence instigated by Filomena, who wanted to test the constancy of Slavuron's love (like any heroine in medieval romance), our hero manages to win the hand of his beloved. But the story does not end with the wedding. The couple's baby son mysteriously disappears and we later learn that the child had been stolen by the high priest (Constantinople was apparently a pagan city at the time), who has fallen in love with the fair Filomena. According to the law of the land, Filomena must spend three nights in the temple in order to expiate her supposed crime of losing the child, and while she is in the temple the persistent high priest attempts to ravish her. Slavuron, who had prudently secreted himself in the temple to protect his wife, kills the priest. For the crime of desecrating the temple the Slav, his Greek wife and their young daughter are eventually exiled. They go to Rus' and receive an honorable welcome from the Slavic ruler. Slavuron, who had risen to become a high military commander in Constantinople, receives the same post in Rus'. Several years pass, and Filomena dies. One night Slavuron comes across his daughter with a young newcomer on the grounds of his house, and in a rage kills the young man. Almost at once he discovers that the young man had been his own long-lost son. His daughter commits suicide. Slavuron then loses his post and is forced to live alone in exile for the rest of his days.[31]

Slavuron's story will serve to indicate the general tenor of large sections of Ladon's narrative. The remainder of it is in fact taken up with the story of Askalon, the arch-villain of the piece, which is nar-

[30] Slavuron's story begins in *Peresmešnik*, I, 187 and ends at II, 54.

[31] The motif of a father unknowingly killing his son is not uncommon. It forms a famous section in Firdausi's Persian epic *Shahname*, wherein the hero Rustem kills his son Sohrab. In the manuscript tale "Eruslan Lazarevič" the confrontation between father and son is introduced, but the tragedy is avoided: father and son recognize each other, and at the end the son sets off on adventures which will obviously be similar to those of his father.

rated to Siloslav by a spirit named Svida. Before he starts his story, Svida takes Siloslav to a terrifying place under the ground, a foretaste of hell itself, and shows him the torments of Askalon, now turned into the centaur-like creature Polkan. Siloslav also witnesses torments of all kinds being inflicted upon other sinners in a passage which recalls other guided tours of hell in literature, particularly those of the *Aeneid* and Dante's *Inferno*, as well as one of the most famous Apocrypha in Russia, "The Descent of the Virgin into Hell" (Xoždenie Bogorodicy po mukam"), a work that Čulkov must certainly have known. The sinners are cast into a river of fire which is surrounded by bitter cold and permanent frost and snow. When they attempt to flee the flames they find they cannot endure the icy cold, and so they leap back once again into the fiery river.

The demonic Askalon falls in love with Askliada, who loves Alim, a foundling who predictably enough discovers at the end of the tale that he is a prince. Alim returns Askliada's love. It is essential of course that Alim and Askliada be separated. The search of the hero for his beloved was the mainstay of the French heroic novel. This plot line, such as it is, enables the author to engage his hero in a series of adventures and travels to exotic places, at the end of which he always finds his beloved and everlasting happiness. Alim has the misfortune to attract the attentions of a goddess Aropa (she is another of Čulkov's inventions), and when he rejects her advances, she inflicts a series of trials upon him: he is swallowed by a fabulous sea monster, changed into an eagle, and finally into a tree. Ironically, it is Askalon who manages to save Alim, this time with a talismanic stone, but Askalon at once falls in love with Askliada and so the trials of the young lovers begin anew.

The Faustean Askalon is willing to commit any crime in order to possess Askliada and he sells his soul (it is not quite put in these terms) to the devils and demons, who promise to help him gain possession of Askliada. With the aid of a magic book that foretells the future and a mirror that will picture anything or anybody he wishes to see (both thoughtfully supplied by the devils), Askalon causes a great deal of harm before he is finally brought to account. The narrator warns us: "This tempestuous man sought not glory, but always ruin for human beings, for he was born under an evil planet, and from his earliest days was determined to bring harm to all mortals." [32]

The narrative is therefore made up of a complex blend of influences,

32 *Peresmešnik*, IV, 126 (incorrectly numbered 266 in the third edition).

and this complexity may, in part at least, be traced to the special circumstances of Čulkov's social background and education. The complexity of influences in his work also reflects his cultural environment, for at this period Russian literature as a whole was undergoing an amazingly compressed development after centuries of isolation or partial isolation from Western European literatures. As I have pointed out, Čulkov's modest social origin must be taken into account when we consider the reasons for his choosing to write prose fiction in the first place, and for choosing to write the type of prose fiction he did. Russian neo-classicism certainly colored his outlook but he drew upon sources which were despised or ignored by most of his literary contemporaries. It is instructive to note that the first two writers of prose fiction in Russia were both of non-noble origin: Čulkov and Fëdor Èmin.[33]

One of the most striking features of Ladon's narrative is its magic, fairy-tale quality. Here Čulkov was borrowing no doubt from the Arabian Nights tales, but also from Russian folklore. Certain other parts of Ladon's narrative, particularly the interpolated story of Slavuron's life, suggest that Čulkov was drawing upon native sources. Although this story does of course contain elements familiar in the French heroic novels, it is equally reminiscent of the Russian manuscript tales of the Petrine and post-Petrine period. Slavuron reminds us of the typical talented Russian who travel, makes a successful marriage abroad with a high-born foreigner, and achieves fame and fortune. However, as we have seen, Slavuron's story does not end at this point and he is forced to leave Constantinople.

This feature of the so-called Petrine tales brings us to the question of the contribution made by Čulkov to the various traditions from which he borrowed in Ladon's narrative. It consists of Čulkov's substitution of a Slavic Pantheon of gods and goddesses for those of Classical Antiquity. There can be no doubt that he was familiar with Russian folk tales and also with some of the early chronicles, if only through the *Sinopsis* of Innokentij Gizel' (and the historical researches of Lomonosov).[34] Čulkov repeatedly mentions pagan Slavic temples where

[33] The aristocratic defenders of the novel at the Cadet School tried to make a case for it in the same terms they would have employed for any genre: they stressed its moralizing import. Xeraskov wrote the first of this three didactic novels in the manner of Fénelon in 1768: *Numa, ili procvetajuščij Rim (Numa, or Rome Flourishing).*

[34] In his poem "Stixi na Semik", published in Week 22 of his journal *I to i së*, Čulkov recalls the ancient pagan customs of the Slavs before the idol Perun was

certain Slavic deities were worshipped, instead of introducing the ancient Greek and Roman gods. He does, however, comment at one point that the Slavs traveled widely as both warriors and merchants, were familiar with the Greek gods, and did not object to worshipping in their temples.[35] Čulkov is careful to explain the parts played by these pagan deities in the pre-Christian Slavic religion. He does this by drawing comparisons with the deities of Classical Antiquity, which he also uses in the normal way like any neo-classical writer of the period. For example, having explained in a footnote that Svetovid or Svjatovič had a temple at Akhrona (on the island of Rügen) and was the Slavic god of the sun and of war, he goes on at once to attempt a comparison with Phoebus.[36]

Čulkov puts the Slavic gods and goddesses to work; that is, he has them perform the same sort of functions that the deities performed in Classical literature. For example, Perun (god of lightning, leader of the Slavic Pantheon, equivalent to Zeus) at one point ordains that the hero Kidal shall be the savior of the city of Xotyn', and all the characters concerned realize at once that this will surely come to pass. We have already given the example of the goddess Aropa falling in love with Alim and taking a direct part in the action of the narrative. This goddess is unknown to students of Slavic mythology, as is another called Zimcerla, whom Čulkov likens to Aurora and says had a temple in Kiev at one time; this seems to be pure invention. Čulkov did actually create some parts of his Pantheon; others he took over from earlier sources, making the same errors they had made. But what is important is not merely the accuracy of Čulkov's Pantheon, but its introduction into literature as a substitute for the Classical Pantheon.

It is Zimcerla and Svetovid that Čulkov uses on occasion in peri-

cast into the water, thus showing that he was aware of the historical fact that the Grand Duke St. Vladimir ordered all the idols to be cast into the River Dnieper when he introduced Christianity as the Kievan state's official religion. Čulkov also notes in this poem that the names of the old pagan gods sometimes occur in popular songs, and even quotes one.

[35] *Peresmešnik*, III, 79.

[36] *Peresmešnik*, I, 162-164. Čulkov later expanded his footnote about Svetovid in his *Abevega russkix sueverij* (Moscow, 1786), pp. 286-291. Čulkov, and also his friend Mixail Popov, seem to have been fascinated by Slavic mythology and its literary possibilities. Čulkov displayed an early interest in mythology in his *Kratkoj mifologičeskoj leksikon*, which was published in 1767.

The temple Čulkov mentions did in fact exist at Arkona; it was described by Saxo Grammaticus in *Gesta Danorum*, XIV (1208). See Marija Gimbutas, "Ancient Slavic Religion: A Synopsis", *To Honor Roman Jakobson*, I (Mouton, The Hague and Paris, 1967), p. 739.

phrastic descriptions of dawn and dusk, again imitating Classical literature: "When the winds calmed and the storm began to die down, then crimson Zimcerla rose in the sky and shining Svetovid following her warmed the earth." [37] A more flippant instance of Čulkov's literary use of Slavic deities occurs when a courtier named Boman attempts to disarm his niece into having an affair with him by pointing to the sexual relations among the Slavic gods Perun and Lada and others, all of whom belonged to the same family. Čulkov was here trying to parallel the scandalous behavior of the Greek gods and goddesses.[38]

I spoke earlier in this chapter of the two broad traditions of narrative prose fiction that could be discerned in seventeenth-century France and in the manuscript tales that were popular in Russia during the first half of the eighteenth century. I also noted that of the two traditions, the older one – that of the heroic novel and idealized romance – was of course better established, and hence dominated. Ladon's narrative, which I have been discussing thus far, belongs to this dominant tradition, and furthermore it occupies well over two-thirds of *The Mocker,* so that at least the proportions of Čulkov's work reflect faithfully enough the relative positions of the two traditions: there is nothing 'mocking' about the greater part of *The Mocker*. Ladon's narrative contains some interesting episodes, but it is on the whole too obviously derivative. Far more successful are those parts of the work narrated by the young monk, and incidentally the frame story, which is narrated by Ladon.

The frame story and the parts of *The Mocker* narrated by the monk are, broadly speaking, representative of the satirical and anti-romance tradition, to which reference was made earlier in this chapter. This tradition is best exemplified in seventeenth-century France by Charles Sorel's novel *La vraie histoire comique de Francion* (1623-33) and Paul Scarron's *Le roman comique* (1651-1657). Hence, Čulkov's work might be used to illustrate the development of prose fiction in microcosm, certainly of the prose fiction in his own country. It is one of the axioms of Russian scholarship that in the eighteenth century Russian literature underwent a compressed development during which it absorbed willy-nilly a bewildering variety of influences, as the country itself sought to assume its rightful role among the European community of nations. Čulkov would serve as an excellent example of the truth of this scholarly axiom.

[37] *Peresmešnik*, I, 185.
[38] *Peresmešnik*, IV, 62.

Unlike Ladon, the young monk does tell a number of separate tales, as he had promised the fair and disconsolate Alenona. He tells five short stories in the second volume of *The Mocker*, then in the third volume begins a quite long narrative entitled "The Tale of the Origin of the Taffeta Beauty Spot ("Skazka o roždenii taftjanoj muški"), which is not finally completed until the fifth and last volume of the tales. The fifth volume ends with three more short stories which are presumably narrated by the monk, but this is not made clear.[39] Once again, as with Ladon's narrative, we find Čulkov drawing upon a variety of sources, both foreign and domestic, with the former predominating.

The first of the five short stories told by the monk is entitled "The Guessers" ("Ugadčiki") and is an example of the riddle motif, which is a feature of some Russian folk tales and at times was incorporated into manuscript tales of serious import. For example, in the sixteenth-century "Tale of Peter and Fevronia" the young woman Fevronia, who is obviously of modest social background, speaks in riddles which the servants of Prince Peter are unable to resolve.[40] Although it seems that this tale told by the monk does owe something to native influences, we must note that the story is set in Turkey and it is a Kadi, or Moslem judge, who finally manages to guess which of three sons had stolen their father's inheritance in order to deprive the other two of their rightful share.

The second story is called "The Protégé" ("Stavlennik"). It is of immediate interest because it has a contemporary theme and is set in provincial Russia, just like the frame story. Instead of the heathen priests (*žrecy*) of Ladon's narrative, here we have a story about the death of an Orthodox priest (*svjaščennik*) and the attempt of a bishop to find a replacement. The tone throughout is ironical, as in the frame story, and presents an immediate contrast to the solemn tone that is maintained in Ladon's narrative. The story opens as follows: "In a certain noble's village the priest departed to his brethren, the Orthodox who here and in all the world lie asleep, or more simply, he died. The nobleman, his peasants, and in a word all the metaphorical sheep were

[39] The first five tales and the last three tales narrated by the monk, as well as the frame story, are included in *Russkaja proza XVIII veka*, I (Moscow-Leningrad, 1950), pp. 89-156. Regrettably, the monk's long tale is not included and has not been reprinted since the eighteenth century; it is probably the single most interesting piece in the whole work, as I hope to show later.

[40] "Povest' o Petre i Fevronii", in *Xrestomatija po drevnej russkoj literature XI-XVII vekov*, 5th ed. rev., ed. N. K. Gudzij (Moscow, 1952), pp. 236-244.

left without a shepherd." [41] The language is deliberately archaic and Čulkov is in fact parodying a part of the Russian Orthodox Liturgy ("Molitva priležnogo molenija"). The anti-clerical tone and the parodying were common features of the Russian seventeenth-century satirical tales.[42] This story is a sharp, but not heavy-handed, satire on the ignorance of the Russian provincial clergy. The bishop decides to test the qualifications of the local sexton for the recently vacated position of village priest. He asks him to write out briefly what Lucian, Phaedrus and Plutarch had to say in their works. The sexton is at a complete loss and believes that the bishop is speaking about people he knows in the village named Luk'jan and Fëdor, and also a rogue (in Russian: *plut*).

Of the remaining stories in this group of five, only the fourth, which is entitled "The Magnanimous Cuckold" ("Velikodušnyj rogonosec"), contains features which may be reasonably traced to the native manuscript tradition, but its debt to foreign models is probably greater. A servant who has stolen some money and purchased the charms of a fine society lady, tells a gentleman all about his amazing adventure; how he had 'practiced amorous ceremonies' (*upražnjalsja v ljubovnyx ceremonijax*) while his mistress' husband played the violin outside the room. The comical clumsiness of the phrase recalls those attempts at erotic finesse in the French manner which we sometimes find in the earlier Russian tales. For example, in "Frol Skobeev" there occurs a similar phrase: "And the whole night through they enjoyed themselves with corporeal amusements" (*I veselilis' črez vsju noč' telesnymi zabavami*).[43] In both tales a confrontation between the guilty man and the man who has been offended takes place after a church service; this seems to add a certain piquancy to the episode. In "Frol Skobeev" it is the outraged father who comes face to face with Frol outside the Cathedral of the Assumption in the Kremlin; Frol has seduced and then abducted the daughter in order to marry her. The amoral Frol Skobeev finds a more recognizable successor in the person of the young student

[41] *Russkaja proza XVIII veka*, I, p. 132: "U nekotorogo dvorjanina v sele otošël svjaščennik k bratii zde ležaščim i povsjudu pravoslavnym, a prostee umer, ostalsja gospodin, krestjane i slovom, vse slovesnye ovcy bez pastyrja." This is a parody of part of the Orthodox Liturgy, a "Sugubaja ektenija" which contains the phrase: "Ešče molimsja ... o vsex preždepočivšix otcex i bratijax, zde ležaščix i povsjudu, pravoslavnyx."

[42] The best-known example is a tale in which various parts of the church liturgy are parodied: "Prazdnik kabackix jaryžek", in Gudzij, *op. cit.*, pp. 465-470.

[43] Gudzij, *op cit.*, p. 424.

Neox in "The Tale of the Origin of the Taffeta Beauty Spot". There is a definite kinship in the heedless roguery of both characters, who pursue their goal of financial success with single-minded devotion and achieve it by the same route: a wealthy daughter. There is an important difference between the two rogues, and that is their social position. Although he is impecunious and will do anything to get what he wants, Frol is a nobleman; Neox, on the other hand, is nothing more than a poor student and a social climber, and consequently he really belongs to another tradition.

The echoes of earlier Russian manuscript tales in the frame story and in the monk's tales are few, and indeed it would be doing Čulkov less than justice to insist too much on their influence, although it is perfectly obvious that he knew the tales well, because he has moved a great deal further in narrative technique, far beyond anything that one can find in them. One can simply note the echo of some episodes. Much of the content of the frame story and of the tales narrated by the young monk obviously owes a good deal to foreign influences. However, many of the characters and themes exploited by Čulkov can hardly be traced to any specific Western European source. Some were a part of the literary baggage of the eighteenth-century writer in Europe or of the migratory international tales. For example, in the frame story we find the lover pretending to be dead or playing the part of a ghost or devil in order to scare away inquisitive neighbors; the young widow who is so easily and quickly pacified by a gallant young man after laying her elderly husband to rest; and finally the gay, renegade young monk who abandons the cloister and goes out into the world to enjoy a series of picaresque adventures, most of which are of an amorous and roguish nature. Such characters as these, and several others that appear in the frame story and in the monk's tales, can be found in countless works of this and earlier periods.[44]

Hence, *The Mocker* contains both romance and anti-romance. However, it is important to note that Čulkov took obvious pains to keep the narratives of Ladon and the monk separate. That is, he guarded against a confusion of genres and styles as a good neo-classicist would. In Ladon's tales a lofty tone is maintained throughout and the settings are universally unrealistic in their exquisiteness and magical elements. The characters too are all of noble birth, and for the most part of royal family, even when, as in the case of Alim, they are foundlings and no

[44] The point is made by V. V. Sipovskij in his *Očerki po istorii russkogo romana* (St. Petersburg, 1909), pp. 620-621.

one knows what their lineage is until towards the end of the narrative. They move in a world similar to that of French neo-classical tragedy and the popular romances, a world inhabited by kings, queens, and nobles. No one of vulgar origin ever appears and 'the people' serve merely to reflect the emotions that the narrator presumably wishes his reader to experience. As befits a solemn narrative, there is no comedy.

On the other hand, in the frame story and in the monk's tales, the tone is entirely different, chiefly because of the narrator's digressions and comments on the action and on the characters. The magical elements disappear and we find ourselves in real cities such as St. Petersburg or in the Russian provinces. The characters are no longer kings and queens, but servants, merchants, students, village priests, and so on. In Ladon's narrative the reader (or listener) is naturally meant to take the characters seriously and he can never be sure whether a certain episode will end tragically for the character or characters concerned. But in the monk's tales the reader does not take the characters seriously, as is always the case in comic narratives. The student Neox gets into some scrapes, but we are never concerned for we know that he will emerge from them unscathed or at least not much the worse for wear.

I have spoken of the dual traditions of narrative prose upon which Čulkov was able to draw. While it would not be true to say that these two narrative manners – the heroic or idealistic and the burlesque or 'roguish' – are employed as elements in a consistent structural pattern in *The Mocker*, nevertheless they are present, and the monk's tales frequently echo episodes in those of Ladon in a parodical manner. The reader can hardly avoid making comparisons: he is being shown two views of human behavior, with two different narrative angles of vision.

Let us take for example the final story of the first group of five tales narrated by the monk. It is entitled "The Devil and the Desperate Lover" ("D'javol i otčajannyj ljubovnik").[45] Here a devil plays a leading, even a decisive, part in the plot, as do the supernatural beings of the Slavic Pantheon in Ladon's heroic and gallant tales, but the atmosphere is quite different. It recalls more than anything some of the early Ukrainian tales by Gogol' in its extravagant and grotesque quality. The story opens as follows: "In ancient times devils were far bolder than they are today; in those days they used to carry out great pranks not only in houses, but also right out in the streets . . .". This reads

[45] *Russkaja proza XVIII veka*, p. 141.

almost like a direct comment on the preceding narrative by Ladon, as do later events in the tale. A devil comes across a young man who has just had his face slapped by his beloved. The devil happens to be in a good mood and so he asks the man to tell him about himself and his problems. The unfortunate young man replies that he is from the city of Astraxan', the son of a wealthy wine merchant who had indulged him when he was young. In a fit of anger he had killed his father, but then escaped scot free. A nobleman friend persuaded him to go to Moscow, where he spent his inheritance lavishly. The nobleman introduced him to an attractive young lady and he had attempted in vain for two years to win her favors with many luxurious gifts. When he had dissipated all his funds in this way, the woman sent him off with a slap in the face. The reader can see for himself what the young man has not seen, that he has been duped by the nobleman and the woman, eighteenth-century confidence tricksters: hence, this is an example of dramatic irony. The devil decides to do what he can to help.

He plays a number of tricks upon the nobleman until the latter at last goes mad and dies. After tormenting the woman, the devil allows her to be married to the young man, who has not yet overcome his infatuation for her (a nice touch). In spite of the opening reference to 'ancient times', the story seems to be set in Čulkov's own times, and the references to Russian place names such as Moscow and Astraxan', and to the hero's merchant origin are of some interest as instances of Čulkov's Russification of his material, although one should not overemphasize this process of Russification since references to Russian towns are quite common in the seventeenth-century satirical manuscript tales. However, the main point that concerns us here is the parodical aspect of the story. It shows us the reverse side of the coin of 'life' (or literature) from that visible in Ladon's narrative. The other side is portrayed with almost as much fabulous detail and extravagance as Ladon lavishes upon his world of chivalrous knights and virtuous maidens, but the extravagance is not taken at face value: it is the ironical commentary that sets the tone.

Another case in point is the fourth story of this group entitled "The Magnanimous Cuckold" ("Velikodušnyj rogonosec"). A servant in St. Petersburg steals some money, and since he is not accustomed to having large sums of money, he is at first at a loss to know how to spend it. However, the narrator points out that "since the devil is constantly on the alert and meddles in all sorts of things in order to ruin man, he joined up with him and began to incline him not toward good deeds, but toward bad deeds".[46] Of course, one may say that the devil is simply doing his job, but the important point is that the comical reference to the devil's baneful activities is poking fun at the attribution of human motivations to supernatural beings, whether they be devils or gods and goddesses, as in Ladon's narrative.

The partings of lovers in Ladon's tales, and they are legion, are usually attended by lamentations on the part of both hero and heroine. We find an ironical comment on this aspect of the heroic or 'romance' tradition in this same story. The servant resolves to spend some of his new wealth on purchasing the charms of a fine society lady. He quickly comes to an understanding with a certain lady, who closets herself with the young man in her boudoir, leaving a message for her husband that she is ill and should not be disturbed. At the wife's request the considerate husband plays the violin outside her door to soothe her nerves. On the third day the lovers have to part and the narrator adds: "If I had been with them at the time, then of course I would not have let the occasion go by without composing an elegy; however, they parted in prose without any verse whatsoever."[47]

From these examples it can be seen that it is not only the difference in the settings of the episodes and in the social station of the characters that serves to distinguish the narratives of Ladon and the young monk, and that provides opportunities for satire and parody, but also, and very importantly, the difference in narrative tone. In his stories Ladon accepts the characters at their own estimation of themselves; he gives us no angle of vision on events and characters. A further difference between the two narratives is that there are very few digressions or asides in Ladon's narrative (the frame story is of course excluded), and those that do exist are not too imaginative. Apart from rather wooden pronouncements to the effect that love is blind, we find only occasional periphrastic descriptions of dusk and dawn in the Classical manner and, more rarely, some examples of the pathetic fallacy. When the heroine Askliada's body is discovered in a grove (she will be resuscitated so that the story can go on), we are told: "The sun, it is said, stopped at that time and changing its bright radiance into bloody and gloomy rays, was amazed at this sight and sympathized with the grief of the people."[48] Asides play a far more important role in the frame story

[46] *Russkaja proza XVIII veka*, p. 138.
[47] *Russkaja proza XVIII veka*, pp. 139-140.
[48] *Peresmešnik*, IV, III. We note that "the people" occur very rarely in these

and the tales narrated by the monk. They cover a broad range of subject matter and are generally satirical or ironical in tone.[49]

It is no easy task to show where Čulkov came from, as it were, which is what I have sought to do in this chapter. *The Mocker* is a potpourri concocted of various themes and narrative styles. Čulkov drew upon both domestic and foreign sources, but the latter seem to have dominated, and in any case the Russian manuscript tales were themselves in the main borrowed from Western European models. In both foreign and domestic prose fiction he found two broad traditions and these are fairly well represented in *The Mocker*. Ladon's narrative belongs to the older tradition of the romance and is rather derivative; apart from the introduction of a Slavic pantheon of mythological gods and goddesses, some of them invented, it contains little that is new. The narrative manner is bland and there are only occasional asides. On the other hand, in the frame story and the monk's tales, which also owe a great deal to Western European fiction, Čulkov has been able to do much with his material. He shows a freshness of approach which looks forward to later Russian prose rather than backwards to the older romance.

---

tales and then only as a muted chorus. Citizens are always completely devoted to their rulers, sharing their joys and sorrows, apparently having none of their own.

[49] This matter of narrative tone is discussed more fully in Chapter IV.

III

ČULKOV'S SATIRICAL JOURNALS

After publishing the first four parts of *The Mocker*, Čulkov continued to pay his debt to the two main traditions of prose fiction that were popular during that period. If his short novel about the tragic love affair of Achilles, *The Adventure of Achilles Under the Name of Pyrrha Before the Siege of Troy*, represented a continuation of the romance tradition familiar to us already from Ladon's narrative, then Čulkov's first satirical journal, *This and That*, published in the same year 1769, for the most part belongs to the burlesque or anti-romance tradition, exemplified in the tales told by the young monk and in the frame story.[1] The bulk of the material in this journal, both prose and verse, was written by Čulkov himself, although it does contain fairly sizable contributions from Aleksandr Sumarokov and Mixail Popov, and possibly others who have not been identified: the material is hardly ever signed.[2] In the journal we find in both theme and narrative technique several features which we met in *The Mocker*.

Čulkov's *This and That* was the second of several satirical journals that appeared in 1769. Like the other weekly and monthly publications, it was in fact a direct response to the first journal, *Hodgepodge* (*Vsjakaja vsjačina*), edited by Grigorij Kozickij, private secretary to the Empress Catherine II. It soon became an open secret that the Empress herself was responsible for a considerable part of the journal's contents and for its editorial policy. Given the uncommon speed with which Čulkov apparently began producing his journal at the end of January,

[1] Each weekly issue consisted of eight unnumbered pages. In the United States the journal *I to i së* is available only at the Library of Congress. Brief selections from the journal (Weeks 1, 3, 5, 28) may be found in L. B. Lextblau, *Russkie satiričeskie žurnaly XVIII veka: izbrannye stat'i i zametki* (Moscow, 1940).

[2] Two letters in Week 5 and the whole of Week 6 belong to Sumarokov. Popov contributed numerous poems in Weeks 7, 12, 18-21, 31. His contributions were reprinted in a collection of his works: M. Popov, *Dosugi, ili Sobranie sočinenij i perevodov*, 2 vols. (St. Petersburg, 1772). See L. N. Majkov, *Neskol'ko dannyx dlja istorii russkoj žurnalistiki* (St. Petersburg, 1876), p. 27.

it may well be that he had some prior knowledge of Catherine's intention to publish her own journal and encourage her loyal subjects to follow her lead.

The title, epigraph, and much of the opening issue of Čulkov's journal are transparently inspired by those of Catherine's. The titles of both journals could be translated in very similar terms. On the first page of *Hodgepodge* we find: "I offer this issue with my compliments, but kindly buy the following issues" (*Sim listom b'ju čelom; a sleduju ščija vpred' izvol' pokupat'*). On Čulkov's first page we have an obvious echo of this phrase: "I serve with lines, I offer paper with my compliments; kindly buy both, and having bought them, regard them as a gift, for they cost very little" (*Strokami služu, bumagoj b'ju čelom, a oboe voobšče izvol'te pokupat', kupiv že sdelajte za podarok, dlja togo, čto nebol'šogo onoe stoit*).[3] Catherine's journal opens with grandiloquent good wishes to its readers for a happy New Year, and Čulkov also congratulates his countrymen on the same occasion in exaggeratedly florid terms.

In his response to *Hodgepodge* and in the ensuing dialogue which took place between him and Catherine, we can discern the same bantering tone which is so striking a feature of the narrative of the young monk in *The Mocker*. Catherine soon welcomed her 'grandson' on the pages of *Hodgepodge*, but displayed some irritation: ". . . our first born son was ungrateful to his mother, for quite disrespectfully he called her his elder sister; we do not mention his many other acts against his mother. We will say no more about this family quarrel".[4] This was an obvious reply to a letter included by Čulkov in his third issue. He began Week 3 with a proverb: "Well begun is half done" (*Kto xorošo načal, tot polovinu dela sdelal*), and then admitted that he had not followed his own precept – a good example of the undercutting narrative technique of which Čulkov was so fond. He addressed his letter to 'Milady, Madame *Hodgepodge*' (the Russian title is in the feminine gender), requesting that she not be angry with him if he calls her his sister – an elder sister since she had "come into the world earlier from nature's womb" – and asked her forgiveness for not having greeted her in the

[3] Čulkov adds a Latin tag, which apparently has no special significance: *Concordia res parvae crescunt, discordia magnae dilabuntur* ("From agreement small things grow, but from discord (even) large things are destroyed"). V. V. Tuzov, editor of the journal *Daily (Poden'šina)*, made fun of Čulkov's use of Latin.

[4] *Vsjakaja vsjačina* (St. Petersburg, 1769), p. 74. Like many of the journals of this period, Catherine's has not been reprinted. I consulted a copy in the Rare Book Division of the Library of Congress.

first issue of his own journal. The letter is signed 'Your obedient brother and servant'. Čulkov adopted a characteristically self-deprecatory manner and declined politely but firmly to indulge in the type of moralizing satire urged by the Empress. Catherine, in encouraging the publishing of journals by private citizens, was anxious that any satire they contained should be directed against universal moral faults, such as greed, avarice, and the like, very much in the manner of the seventeenth-century neo-classical satire in France. It is for this reason that she became impatient with men like Nikolaj Novikov, who insisted on directing their satire against real and genuine faults in contemporary Russian society, such as the stupidity and bestiality of provincial landowners and the brutal maltreatment of serfs. Čulkov's satire was not of either variety; it was mostly literary. In his letter to *Hodgepodge* he confessed that he could not take it upon himself to instruct others: "I cannot make so bold as to assume the title of teacher of the nation, because I am unworthy and besides I cannot teach people since I am a pretty middling sort of fellow myself" (*i sam serëtka na polovine*). It is of course this refusal to pontificate, to moralize, which is one of the most refreshing characteristics of Čulkov's literary outlook. In his repeated declarations that he sought only to entertain, not to instruct, Čulkov was running counter to one of the prevailing views of literary endeavor, held by Catherine herself, as well as by Sumarokov and Novikov, even though these three by no means agreed on all points about the purposes of literature.

Given the difference in their views and purposes, it was natural that the relations between Čulkov and Catherine, at least as editors of satirical journals, should not run smoothly. On only one occasion did Čulkov take a step towards the type of universal satire which was advocated by Catherine, and even then one suspects that he was really seeking a brief alliance against the other journals, particularly those of Novikov and Èmin. In Week 23 (June) Čulkov addressed a second letter to Catherine, this time making little effort to disguise the fact that he knew she was directing the editorial policy of the journal *Hodgepodge*, and signing himself "Weekly" (*Eženedel'nik*). He wrote that he was prepared to follow her 'judicious and unbiased discourses upon human characteristics', even if this occasioned the hostility of others. He felt encouraged to publish satirical descriptions of Russian *petits-maîtres*. These satirical descriptions are of a routine nature, directed against dandies who get up at two in the afternoon and like the moon appear to the world only at dusk. Čulkov's satire recalls that of other

Russian writers on the same theme, which was quite popular at the time. His sketches of certain types of dandies with names such as Narcissus, Chameleon, and Harlequin remind us of those of Kantemir, whose satires had been published in Russia for the first time in 1762. Čulkov does not go back on his refusal to moralize, but he does on this occasion follow Catherine's line on satire by directing his aim at such politically harmless subjects as Gallomania and dandyism. His mention of the hostility that his decision might provoke may be taken almost certainly as a jibe at Novikov, who in his journal *Drone* (*Truten'*), which began to appear in May, championed a sharply pointed satire with socio-political overtones, directed against specific targets in Russian contemporary life.

However, Čulkov must soon have had a change of heart, for the following month in Week 28 he attacked *Hodgepodge*, together with *Drone* and Èmin's monthly *Infernal Mail* (*Adskaja počta*), which began to appear in July. Čulkov published a letter from a mysterious 'D.P.', who had decided to request a correspondence with him after rejecting the other journals for various reasons. Perhaps as a safeguard, since his criticism of Catherine's journal is very blunt, Čulkov has his correspondent say he does not know him. 'D.P.' had thought of writing to *Hodgepodge*, the oldest journal (*pramater'* 'great grandmother'), but it has already grown old and weak-minded.[5] He finds *Drone* is the enemy of all humanity, full of curses and crude attacks on people; perhaps the author himself suffers from the sins he keeps attacking? He wants nothing to do with evil spirits and so he will avoid *Infernal Mail*.

It is interesting to see that when Čulkov resumed his satire against *Hodgepodge* some months later in Week 45 (November), he chose one of his favorite weapons: parody. He began by announcing that he had decided to follow the example of others and write himself a letter praising his own journal. Čulkov made no mention of Catherine's journal, but his readers undoubtedly understood that he had it in mind rather than any other. Catherine published many letters purporting to come from admirers and telling of the highly complimentary opinion held of the journal by everyone.[6] Čulkov's letter is a delightful parody. His 'correspondent' lavishes comical praise on *This and That* and declares that he can hardly contain himself until Tuesday comes around

[5] Catherine herself anonymously referred to *Hodgepodge* as *prababka*, "great-grandma".

[6] There were a number of attacks on the self-congratulatory letters that appeared so often in Catherine's journal. A rather blunt attack occurs in a journal edited by Vasilij Ruban, *Ni to ni së*, List 5, March 21.

and he can buy the journal: "My heart is filled with sweetness, when fair Aurora shows her nose on the horizon, and winged Time strides ahead of her and writes above us *Tuesday*." [7] He sighs with pleasure after reading every line, his blood runs cold at each period. Then Čulkov has his fictitious correspondent give a sharp dig at Catherine's pretensions and her confidence that she was correcting manners in her journal: ". . . you have corrected our rough manners and shown us that one must eat when one feels hungry. Your philosophy has also taught us that if a man does not have a horse, then he must assuredly go on foot." Here Čulkov suggests that Catherine's moralizing satire simply states the obvious: virtues are good, vices are bad.

Čulkov's editorial disagreements with other journals, such as the one with Catherine which we have been examining, do of course enable us to get a fairly clear idea of where he stood on certain literary matters, and the manner in which he chose to conduct the argument confirms in large measure what we already know of the preference he had for certain satirical and parodical modes. This preference led him early in his career to make extensive use of the burlesque.

Paul Scarron's *Virgile travesti* became the first and best-known example of the low burlesque in Europe; in it the Classical heroes and their feats are described in a deliberately vulgar and degrading style. Boileau was offended by this degrading type of poem, and with his own work *Le Lutrin* introduced the high burlesque or what he called a 'Poème héroï-comique". In a foreword to the reader Boileau explained that he sought to portray low characters and events in an elevated style. Although terminology varied, Boileau's influence was such that the high burlesque, or mock-heroic poem, came to be preferred in both France and England. However, in Russia Sumarokov, the chief proponent of Boileau's views, displayed some independence in this matter. In a major statement of his views in 1748 (the epistle "On Poetry") he resolved to give his blessing to both types of burlesque, high and low. Sumarokov in his epistle gives some examples of the low burlesque and then explains: "In this type (of burlesque) lines dealing with lofty deeds are written in a very low style." After giving examples of the high burlesque, or mock-heroic, he again explains: "In this type the Muse must

[7] Also typical of Čulkov in this parody is his use of mythological references. Aurora is degraded by the burlesque phrase about popping her nose over the horizon.

provide lofty words for low actions." [8] Sumarokov does not suggest that either type of burlesque is to be preferred. The first burlesque poem published in Russia was, however, the high type advocated by Boileau. This was Majkov's mock-heroic poem *The Ombre Player* which appeared in 1763.[9] In terms of an epic battle it tells the story of a card game. A young man about town has an unfortunate passion for cards: he gambles and loses.

There can be no doubt that Čulkov knew both Sumarokov's epistle and Majkov's mock-heroic poem, and was operating within a Russian tradition in using the burlesque himself. What distinguishes his use is that it occurs in his prose fiction, although he also wrote some burlesque poems. In his poems, which appeared in his journal *This and That* in 1769, Čulkov employs both high and low burlesque, although in his prose fiction high burlesque definitely predominates. Both types of burlesque depend for their comic effect on the incongruity between subject matter and language, and it is this comic incongruity which became a major feature of Čulkov's prose style, particularly in the frame story and the monk's tales.

Čulkov used the burlesque to satirize and parody others, and we have already had a hint of this in his polemic with the Empress and her journal *Hodgepodge*. He reserved his most elaborate attacks for his favorite target, Fëdor Èmin. It is hard to know who began their fierce battle of words. In any case, Russian writers at this period hardly needed much urging to engage in literary polemic. One is often impressed by the amount of feuding that went on in the eighteenth century. Almost every Russian writer took part and the modern reader of many of their works frequently has the feeling that he is eavesdropping on a series of private quarrels. Čulkov and Èmin were rival producers of prose fiction, and some contemporaries evidently felt that the moralizing in Èmin's novels (or rather, romances) was hypocritical and

[8] "Èpistola II (o stixotvorstve)", in A. P. Sumarokov, *Izbrannye proizvedenija*, 2nd ed. (Leningrad, 1957), p. 123.

[9] Vasilij Majkov, *Igrok Lombera* (Moscow, 1763). The poem enjoyed great popularity in the eighteenth century: a second edition appeared in 1765, a third in 1774, and a fourth in 1783. It belongs to the genre of the game poem, which blossomed in England and elsewhere in Europe following the enormous success of Pope's *The Rape of the Lock*. The third canto of Pope's mock-heroic poem contains the famous description of a game of ombre. Majkov knew no foreign languages, but he may well have heard of Pope's poem at secondhand. In any case his own poem quite obviously belongs to the same tradition; it is surprising to find no mention of this fact in the critical literature.

Ombre was quite a popular game in Russia. Cf. reference to the game of ombre in Puškin's *Evgenij Onegin*, Chapter 5, Canto XXXV.

designed to pander to the taste of highly placed patrons; we need not be surprised that Čulkov objected to this and ridiculed Èmin at every opportunity. The apparent popularity of Èmin's works must have rubbed salt into the wound, as it were, and earned Èmin Čulkov's personal dislike. There certainly appears to be an extra note of bitterness in Čulkov's attacks on Èmin which does not appear in his literary polemics with such men as Sumarokov and Vasilij Majkov. Èmin traveled extensively before appearing at the Russian Embassy in London in 1761. He soon went to Russia and after two years as a tutor and translator began a brief but extremely prolific career as a writer. He died suddenly and rather mysteriously in 1770; we do not know what caused his death (he was thirty-five). Èmin obviously antagonized many of his contemporaries, especially Sumarokov, by boasting of his sojourns in various exotic lands, his unequalled knowledge of European literature and culture, and by announcing his intention to do something to raise the abysmally low standards of Russian literature.

In Week 35 (September) of his journal *This and That* Čulkov published three "Conversations of the Dead". The genre of the dialogue between famous men long since dead was very widely spread in European literature, and no doubt Fontenelle's *Dialogues des Morts* (1683) was well known in Russia. The original, or at least the most famous practitioner of this genre in ancient times, was Lucian, some of whose satirical dialogues were published and also imitated by Sumarokov in his journal *The Industrious Bee*.[10] Sumarokov's dialogues featured both famous dead men and also allegorical figures such as the miser, the thief, and so on. Čulkov followed Sumarokov's example in producing both kinds of conversation and in using the genre as a satirical weapon.[11] In his next issue, Week 36, Čulkov published a conversation between Mercury, Charon, and a character called Zlojazyčnik (Eviltongue), who, it soon becomes clear, is meant to represent Èmin. The messenger of the gods brings Zlojazyčnik to Charon, who makes him drink from the river of oblivion so that he will tell the absolute truth about himself. Zlojazyčnik confesses that he is in fact a poor Ukrainian

[10] *Trudolubivaja pčela* (St. Petersburg, 1759). Some of Lucian's *Dialogues* were translated by "G.K." (possibly Kozickij, who later became private secretary to Catherine).

[11] A Russian scholar has remarked upon the obvious influence of Sumarokov's journal on Čulkov's. Like Sumarokov, Čulkov included translations of Lucian, Ovid, Rabener, and Gellert. See: V. N. Putilov, "O žurnalakh Čulkova (*I to i së i Parnasskij ščepetil'nik*)", *Učënye zapiski Leningradskogo gos. ped. instituta im. A. I. Gercena*, Vol. 29 (1940), 102.

and, in spite of all his protestations of service to Russian society, he wrote only for money. Although Èmin claimed to be the scion of an illustrious and influential Ottoman Turkish family in Istanbul, several people held firmly to the belief that he was in fact a Ukrainian who had traveled abroad and then come back to Russia to make a career for himself by utilizing his knowledge of foreign languages. Both Čulkov and Sumarokov were of this opinion and used it in their frequent satires against Èmin. What is of particular interest in Čulkov's dialogue between Mercury, Charon and Zlojazyčnik is that he has made use of this genre in order to ridicule a rival, and not to make generalized satirical comments on the vanity and foolishness of men, as Sumarokov had done.[12]

It is again Èmin who figures as the chief target in three fairly long burlesque poems that Čulkov published in his journal of 1769. Two of them were printed in the journal and the third and the longest was published as a supplement at the end of the year. The two poems printed in the journal are "Stixi na kačeli" ("Verses on a Ferris wheel") in Weeks 16, 17, and 18 (without title), and "Stixi na *Semik*" in Week 22 (also without title) – *Semik* is a religious holiday celebrated on the Thursday of the seventh week after Easter, equivalent to Whitsun. The third poem, which appeared as a supplement to the journal, is entitled "Plačevnoe padenie stixotvorcev" ("The Poets' Sad Downfall").[13]

In these poems Čulkov spreads his net very wide indeed and we cannot hope to pick up all the references to contemporary figures which occur in them, often taking no more than a line or two. However, Èmin is clearly the major target in Čulkov's longest poem "The Poets' Sad Downfall". It was subtitled, presumably by the author, 'a satirical poem'. The poem is divided into three cantos; the first of 272 lines, including a comic invocation of 38 lines, the second of 392 lines, and the third of 196 lines. With considerable skill Čulkov takes the theme of Èmin's unexpected arrival in Russia, his mysterious origin, his boasting and the hostility it aroused among Russian writers, and transforms it into an extended burlesque, in which a bizarre warrior-poet

[12] The point is made in V. Šklovskij, *Čulkov i Levšin* (Leningrad, 1933), p. 76.
[13] All three poems with titles appeared in 1775 in a separate volume that has neither date nor author's name. There is a copy in the Rare Book Division of the Library of Congress. The poems have been reprinted and are available in volume one of *Poèty XVIII veka*, eds. G. P. Makogonenko and I. Z. Serman, 3d. ed. (Leningrad, 1958). They may also be found in *Russkaja poèzija*, ed. S. A. Vengerov, Vol. I: "XVIII vek. Èpoxa klassicizma" (St. Petersburg, 1897), and in *Iroi-komičeskaja poèma* (Leningrad, 1933).

arrives on Parnassus, creates a disturbance, and earns the ire of Jupiter himself. One wonders whether Čulkov thought of Sumarokov for the part of the irate Jupiter? Sumarokov was notoriously bad-tempered and took his position as law-giver and literary judge very seriously indeed. The warrior-poet eventually brings about his own downfall and that of his following of poetasters by condemning Homer and the epics, a slight which Jupiter simply cannot forgive.

Čulkov opens with a request for divine sympathy because of the dire fate that has befallen Russia's poets:

> Воспой, о Муза, ты теперь плачевным гласом!
> Таким, как волк поет в лесу пред смертным часом,
> Чтоб мать сыра земля услышала твой стон,
> И был бы на гумнах крестьянам внятен он.[14]

The poem is written for the most part in the high burlesque or mock-heroic, but these four lines will illustrate that Čulkov, like most poets, did not write a 'pure' burlesque. He begins in high burlesque, but the reference to 'moist mother earth' is an obvious folklore motif, and the image of the peasants at work is a rather homely one, if not too severely degrading. After a mock request for the Muse's aid in his painful task of describing the poets' downfall from Parnassus, Čulkov suddenly does an about-face and rejects divine assistance. It is typical of Čulkov to surprise us in this way; it is one of his most salient narrative mannerisms. In a neat piece of debunking, which has strong nationalistic overtones, he announces:

> Я от роду воды Кастальской не пивал,
> И пить ее боюсь, что с ног бы не упал,
> Для подкрепления ж восторженного духа,
> Мне лучше кажется российская сивуха.
> . . . .
> А русское вино в нас сердце веселит
> И без Парнаса быть разумными велит.
> Врачебных оных вод хотя не презираю,
> Однако и без них я пети начинаю.[15]

[14] (443) "Sing now, o Muse, with mournful voice! Just as the wolf in the forest sings at the approach of death; So that the moist mother earth may hear your moaning, And that it may be heard by peasants (at work) on the threshing floors." Numbers in parenthesis refer to pages in *Poèty XVIII veka*. The lines are quoted in Cyrillic to avoid the eyestrain of reading transliteration.

[15] (444) "I have never tasted water from the Castalian spring, And I am afraid that if I drink from it, I shall collapse. To strengthen my exalted spirit It is better that I try Russian raw brandy. . . . Russian wine cheers our hearts And bids us be sensible with no need of Parnassus; I do not despise those medicinal waters, But I begin my song without them anyway."

In approved epic fashion Čulkov begins *in medias res*, with the enormous excitement that has been aroused by a rumor about a new planet, an omen of great import. Suddenly a splendid hero appears and, stifling yawns, declares that he has come to amaze all mankind, to bring good to all humanity, and that he will be favored above all others as a writer. He intends to follow no models, only his own inclinations:

Я дам свободный путь пресветлому уму,
И следовать ни в чем не буду никому.
Во всех писателях велики зрю пороки,
Они неправильно свои водили строки.[16]

The second canto opens with an extensive mock-heroic description of the commotion caused by the hero's arrival on Parnassus, but also contains examples of low burlesque in which Jupiter chokes on a melon rind and the gods and goddesses are portrayed as idle peasants who do nothing but eat melon and drink kvas. The warrior-poet and his band of poetasters are put on trial. At the sight of the poets' leader, Clio (the Greek Muse of History) rushes to Jupiter to beg him to avenge the damage done to the subject sacred to her. This is almost certainly a direct satire on Èmin, who had shortly before brought out a history of Russia full of the grossest errors. Not wishing to act hastily, Jupiter asks Apollo to tell him about the poet's behavior on earth. The god of poetry will say not a word (a nice touch), and it is appropriately enough Momus, the god of mockery and censure, who presents the hero's case. Momus acts more the part of prosecutor than that of defender. He says of his client:

Он всех разумнее природу превращает,
И в святки на полях здесь розы насаждает.[17]

These and the following lines hint at the bizarre topography and climatic conditions in Èmin's novels. He mentions Èmin's free adaptations and unacknowledged translation of French works:

Французских авторов, как кисло тесто, месит
И совесть у людей безменами он весит.
Сперва читателей он много удивил,
Понеже не собой, но галлом говорил.[18]

[16] (445) "I shall give free rein to my magnificent mind And I shall emulate no one. I see great faults in all writers, They composed their lines incorrectly."
[17] (458) "He transforms nature more cleverly than anyone, And at Christmas time plants roses here in the fields."
[18] (460) "He kneads French authors like sour dough And weighs people's consciences in a balance. At first he amazed many readers, For he spoke not in his own voice, but in that of a Gaul."

But Momus asserts that the hero's audience was not so gullible as he had hoped and has now assessed him at his true value.

Čulkov also makes an allegation that Èmin was a pie-seller and gives other piquant details of his life in Istanbul, and finally comments on his mysterious birthplace: "He was born in an unknown country – in Ukrainelandia" (*v Xoxlandii*) (462). It should be noted that *xoxol* is a vulgar term for Ukrainian, and furthermore Ukrainians were regarded as provincial in St. Petersburg and Moscow.

The warrior-poet and his band are forgiven and given a second chance, but the third canto of the poem finds them creating mischief on Parnassus once again. More fun is made of Èmin's mysterious origin. Apollo and the Muses plug their ears when the poet begins to recite his verses. He is obviously suffering from a severe case of literary hubris. Not content with tormenting the inhabitants of Parnassus with his own scribbling, he proceeds to condemn out of hand the works of all great writers of the past. When he dismisses Homer's epics as mere trash, Jupiter loses patience: thunder and lightning greet the rash hero's remarks. Jupiter decides to dispense swift justice himself and casts all the poetasters down from Parnassus. The inhabitants of Parnassus may be released from the importuning of bad poets, but there is little hope of peace and quiet for the people on earth. As they are berated, some of the poets are already composing lines for tearful elegies on the subject of their downfall from Parnassus. The poem ends with Čulkov surveying the calm scene among the gods now that the tumult is over.

Čulkov does not limit his attacks to occasional references to Èmin. In parts of his three burlesque poems he gave an extensive critique of many verse genres in favor during that period and parodied some lines from the major poets of Russian neo-classicism – Lomonosov and Sumarokov – and also Vasilij Majkov, a leading disciple of Sumarokov's. In so doing Čulkov appears to have antagonized several people apart from Èmin, notably Sumarokov himself. M. A. Dmitriev, nephew of the poet Ivan Dmitriev, wrote in his memoirs that Čulkov's poems "caused an uproar and created a great deal of resentment against the author among other poets".[19]

The first of the three poems, "Stixi na kačeli", contains the clearest examples of Čulkov's satire on the verse genres practiced by his contemporaries. It consists of two parts: the first and lesser part (222 lines) is narrated by a Poet who tries his hand at various verse genres with a

[19] M. A. Dmitriev, *Meloči iz zapasa moej pamjati*, 2nd ed. (Moscow, 1869).

monotonous lack of success. Once again, even in verse, Čulkov displayed his fondness for the first-person discourse. As the Poet recounts his futile attempts to attain glory by practicing one genre after another, Čulkov is able to satirize certain poets of the time and also to give his own views on the abuses to which the genres involved most readily lend themselves. The poem begins with a mock invocation of the Muse, traditional in the burlesque:

> Скажи, о Муза, мне, как должно начинать,
> Когда о чём-нибудь писатель хочет врать.[20]

But the Muse at once becomes the Poet's grannie (*kuma*), whom he seeks to please with his lines. So that right at the outset we find an example of Čulkov's tendency towards the low or degrading burlesque, in the manner of Scarron.

Čulkov's Poet is at first carried away by the heroic, triumphant ode of the Lomonosov variety, which was also attacked by Sumarokov for its hyperbole and inflated, cosmic imagery.[21] The Poet plays freely with the elements, altering the course of rivers, and boasts:

> Вселенной овладел моими я стихами
> И думал, что уже живу под небесами.[22]

Immediately, without any transition, the Poet continues in a sudden change of tone:

> Потом я затащил в харчевню весь Парнас,
> Минервин на гумне послышался мне глас.[23]

For several lines he shows the Greek gods engaged in a number of low, degrading activities. Hence, he has turned to burlesque or travesty of the ancient epics after an unsuccessful attempt at the inflated ode. Scholars have been struck by the parallels between these lines and others in the poem and some lines in the first canto of *Elisej, or*

[20] (414) "Tell me, o Muse, how a poet should begin, When he wishes to talk nonsense about something."

[21] Lomonosov died in 1765, but his place as a writer of inflated, panegyric odes had been taken by Vasilij Petrov, named by Catherine "a second Lomonosov". Čulkov might well have had him in mind. Petrov translated the *Aeneid* and his version served as the target for many parodies, notably Majkov's *Elisej*. However, it should be noted that Petrov was not a poet without talent; he has been underestimated largely because of the ridicule heaped upon his odes by contemporary poets.

[22] (416) "I mastered the universe with my lines, And thought I was living up above the clouds."

[23] (416) "Then I dragged the whole of Parnassus into an inn; I heard Minerva's voice on the threshing floor."

Bacchus Enraged (*Elisej, ili Razdražënnyj Vakx*), the low burlesque and partial travesty of the *Aeneid* by Vasilij Majkov. These similarities can hardly be pure coincidence, but the problem remains: who was parodying whom? Majkov's poem was not published until 1771, but some scholars have argued that the manuscript of the first parts of the poem dates from as early as 1769, the same year in which Čulkov's own poem was first published in the journal *This and That*.[24] However, the dating of this manuscript is by no means a simple matter, and a controversy over the problem continues to occupy the attention of some Russian scholars. One thing is certain, and that is Čulkov was the first to publish a poem in the low burlesque in Russia, although Sumarokov had sanctioned the low or degrading burlesque as early as 1748 in his epistle "On Poetry". One must admit that it does seem rather unlikely that Čulkov would have taken the trouble to parody some lines of a poem that remained in manuscript. Is it not more reasonable to suppose that Majkov read Čulkov's poem in 1769 and took over some lines from it? Majkov's earlier effort in burlesque had been a mock-heroic poem, that is, in the high burlesque manner: *The Ombre Player* (1763). The view that it was Majkov who copied Čulkov is upheld by G. P. Makogonenko in his introduction to *Poèty XVIII veka*.

Čulkov's Poet soon tires of both heroic and burlesque genres, but does not lose his desire to be a poet: "I abandoned the trumpet and took up the reed-pipe" (417). Čulkov now proceeds to make fun of the writer of sighing love lyrics and pastoral elegies:

Без нужды разогрел мою холодну кровь,
И на досуге я впустил в себя любовь.
Затеял всякий час стопами воздыхати,
Мне вздумалось в стихах для рифмы умирати:
Я в стуки раза три иль больше в ад сходил,
Нередко и свою любовницу водил.[25]

A little later Čulkov criticizes Majkov for considering himself "teacher to half the world", referring obviously enough to Majkov's *Moral Fables and Tales* (*Nravoučitel'nye basni i skazki*), which appeared in

[24] See: A. V. Zapadov, "Žurnal M. D. Čulkova *I to i së* i ego literaturnoe okruženie", *XVIII Vek*, No. 2 (Moscow-Leningrad, 1940), pp. 104-110.

[25] (417) "Needlessly I heated my cold blood And at leisure moments admitted love into my heart. I started sighing in meter at every moment, I thought to die in verse for the sake of rhyme: I descended to hell a couple of times every day, Even taking my beloved with me now and then." I. Z. Serman points to a similarity between the fourth line and a poem of Sumarokov's.

two volumes in 1766 and 1767. Majkov held the view that improvement could result from reading such verses as his. Such a view was naturally calculated to call forth ridicule from Čulkov, who repeatedly declared that literature could not improve morals or manners. A few lines later we find an even more transparent reference to Majkov, or rather to his mock-heroic poem *The Ombre Player*:

> Учиться не хотел, как выступить мне в люди,
> И бубны принимал, не ведая, за жлуди.[26]

The reference is to Leander, hero of the poem, who makes a similar mistake in suits while gambling at cards.

There then follow a number of lines in which the Poet creates a furor on Parnassus by treating its inhabitants as dandies and coquettes who are desperately eager to dress as modishly as possible. Jupiter is disturbed and has the Poet thrashed and chased away. However, the Poet remains as stubborn as ever in his determination to become famous, and he resolves that now he will "surprise the whole world with his eclogues":

> Зимою украшал долины я цветами,
> Медведи за овец паслися там стадами,
> А волки — пастухи, свирели их — хвосты.[27]

The fairy-tale world of the pastoral has been attacked time and again over the centuries in all literatures for its unreality and preciousness, the same faults that Čulkov suggests here. The eclogue was fairly popular in Russia and it is not at all necessary that Čulkov should have had any particular poet in mind. In this case, and in the others also, his prime concern would seem to have been the verse genres themselves, although he was naturally obliged to select specific works for parody and satire.

The Poet is unsuccessful once again and finally despairs of ever achieving fame and fortune through any verse genre. He decides to put up his works for auction, asking his 'grannie' to help him. As his last attempt at verse (he finds it hard to keep his quill dry) he offers a description of the 'kačeli', or Ferris wheel, part of the popular celebration during Easter time.[28] The latter part of the poem (383 lines) is

[26] (418) "I did not want to learn how to behave in society, And in my ignorance took diamonds to be clubs."

[27] (420) "I adorned valleys with flowers in winter, Bears instead of sheep pastured there in flocks, The wolves were shepherds, their tails were pipes."

[28] For a fascinating account of this and other popular amusements of this period

given over to this description, and we leave for some time Čulkov's unsuccessful Poet – Čulkov is now writing from the point of view of a different literary persona, no longer concerned with satirizing poets or parodying verse genres. What is more startling is that in describing the capers of the holiday-makers he employs a high burlesque, a contrast to the prevailing low burlesque of the poem's first part. Čulkov (the description is supposed to have been written by the Poet) portrays people parading, drinking, and dancing in the streets. One drunk blunders into a group of ladies, roughly pushing them and disarranging their holiday finery. The drunk is called 'intoxicated Mars' (*netrezvyj Mars*) and also 'ancient warrior knight' (*drevnij bogatyr'*), recalling the burlesque references in the monk's tales in *The Mocker*. A man soon comes to the ladies' rescue and disposes of the trouble-maker:

> Соперник на земле лежит уже без мочи;
> Не чувства он лишен, но силы только нет,
> И, лежа на земле, отважно вопиет:
> "Постой, — он говорит, — я дам тебе то знати,
> Как должно рыцарей по правам поражати."[29]

Here we have a good example of the mock-heroic or the high burlesque, with the comparison of the episode to a contest of honor among medieval knights in the lists.

All the celebrants get very merry and the Poet wishes them well, bids them enjoy themselves to the full. After a brief mention of a pile of eggs (hinting at the custom of rolling eggs at Easter), Čulkov passes onto a mock-heroic description of the merry-makers falling into the rather murky waters of St. Petersburg's canals. An extended comparison is further developed between a dandy in a cart who drives too fast and is thrown into a wall and injured and Phaethon, the son of Phoebus, who was unable to control the steeds of the sun's chariot and fell to the earth. The story of Phaethon occurs at the beginning of Book II of Ovid's *Metamorphoses*, a work that Čulkov appears to have known well.

After describing the Russian dandies and rakes who, he says, have followed Jupiter's example in changing mistresses every day and in

---

see: Malcolm Burgess, "Fairs and Entertainers in 18th-Century Russia", *The Slavonic and East European Review*, XXXVIII, No. 90 (Dec., 1959), 95-113.

[29] (423) "The rival now lies powerless upon the ground, As yet still conscious but without strength, And as he lay upon the ground he boldly shouted: 'Wait,' said he, 'I will show you How one should strike a knight according to the laws (of chivalry?).'"

taking the most elaborate care of their appearance, Čulkov returns to the Poet of the first part of the poem, who then attempts in desperation a few lines of a triumphal ode and then contradicts himself as Čulkov's other narrators are wont to do:

Природу принуждать не думаю нимало,
И сил во мне к тому нисколько не достало;
Что есть, тому всегда в природе должно быть.[30]

The Poet has heard of people speaking in complimentary terms of such poets as Homer, Vergil, Malherbe, and Pindar, but he does not know their works:

Кто ж Пиндару знаком, пускай тот возьмет лиру
И громко и умно да возвещает миру,
Что солнце из шаров горящих состоит.[31]

Here Čulkov seems to be agreeing with Sumarokov's criticism of the 'loud' Lomonosov, and indeed goes on to parody the poet who makes use of long lists of places and names from Classical mythology, as Lomonosov frequently did. This technique he regards as reaping what one has not sown. Such long lists also became a hallmark of Vasilij Petrov's style.

After a brief mock-heroic description of a brawl, which contains an echo of Russian folklore in the line: "... the bold warrior sat down upon the damp earth" (*k syroj zemle*), Čulkov brings his poem to a close on a serious note. Obviously speaking on his own behalf, he confesses that his verses are uneven, but announces his intention to improve and states he is happy to serve his fellow men: "I dedicate myself to the needs of society" (433).

The poem is, then, rather a mixed bag, as is entirely appropriate for a satire (*satura* in Latin means 'mixed dish'). It contains burlesque (both high and low), satire directed against literary foes and against Gallomania, and a lively description of a popular holiday. This apparently aimless rambling from topic to topic constitutes one of the features of burlesque poems and indeed much satire, as for example Horace and Juvenal, although it is particularly characteristic of Čulkov's narrative technique. The switch from mock-heroic to degrading burlesque and back again is also an essential part of the genre, and has made it almost

[30] (428) "I have no intention of forcing nature, I have not sufficient strength for that; Whatever exists should always be present in nature."
[31] (428) "Whoever knows Pindar, let him take up his lyre And loudly and wisely sing to inform the world That the sun consists of balls of flames."

impossible to establish a fixed terminology for the burlesque in any European literature. As has been pointed out: "... difficulties arise when one attempts to sort out poems and assign them quickly and easily to their proper pigeon-holes. Seldom is a burlesque poem true to type throughout." [32]

Although the content of the poem is motley, its tenor is clear enough. It is a severe and sometimes rather crude criticism of the various types of verse genres being written by his contemporaries, and the first part of the poem contains some rather telling points. One is reminded on several occasions of similar pronouncements on the futile efforts of bad poets by Sumarokov, but Čulkov's poem is much more cheerful and amusing than the embittered and pompous *ex cathedra* decrees of the older poet. Furthermore, Sumarokov himself comes in for his share of ridicule. We have here Čulkov playing the role of literary critic, just as he had done in certain parts of *The Mocker*; this time he criticizes verse, instead of prose, and so he writes in verse, as it were playing the poets at their own game.

To some degree one can say that the switch in styles in the poem, from low to high burlesque, reflects the structure of the work. In the first half of the poem Čulkov uses the low or degrading burlesque in order to criticize the 'high' styles or genres of verse then much in favor. It is the pomposity of Lomonosov's odes, the unnaturalness of Sumarokov's love poems and eclogues, Majkov's moralizing, to which Čulkov takes exception, and it was of course exactly these same faults in their prose equivalents that he objected to and satirized in *The Mocker*. Čulkov was able to stand back from the works of the Russian neoclassical poets and point out their faults with a great deal of common sense, in part because he was essentially a writer of prose himself, but perhaps also because of his close contact with a different type of literature: the folk tales, the popular and down-to-earth humor and the bantering, undercutting irony of Scarron.

In the second half of the poem, having degraded the pompous and lofty styles of poetry then in vogue, Čulkov gives an example of the type of poem he prefers; he was showing the poets what they should select as their themes and how they should write. The contrast presented by his example is of course striking: the carousing of a popular holiday. He announces (still through his Poet) that he "will look closely At all those city squares, where there is an awful twirling And where our unpowdered folk spin around" (421). Surely the thrust of this remark

[32] David Worcester, *The Art of Satire* (Cambridge, Mass., 1940), p. 48.

is essentially away from the pomposity and especially the unnaturalness of the poems of his rivals and towards realism, towards the subject of Russian reality as a right and proper topic for poetry. But Čulkov is able to go only so far in striking new ground, for in describing the popular holiday he uses the mock-heroic; that is, he feels obliged to 'elevate' his 'low' topic.

Čulkov was himself the butt of numerous satires, and those hostile towards him were not slow to make fun of his verse and its occasional clumsiness. The most generous reader could never claim Čulkov as a great poet. Burlesque – high in France, both high and low in Russia – was a perfectly legitimate weapon in the classicist poet's arsenal, and in employing it Čulkov was very much a child of his times. One notes particularly that, in spite of his attempt to introduce new themes in "Stixi na kačeli", and partially in "Stixi na *Semik*" which also describes a popular holiday, the bulk of his verse is in fact very much in the traditional mold. It belongs in the main to the standard satire on bad poets. Čulkov's natural bent as a writer was for the lively, mocking, bantering first-person narrator. He certainly used first-person discourse in parts of all three poems that appeared in his journal *This and That,* but not nearly to the same extent or to the same effect as he was able to do in his prose. His verse, like almost all the Russian verse of the eighteenth century, is curiously impersonal.

Much of the prose material of *This and That* is written from the point of view of the editorial I. This meant that Čulkov was able to gain further practice in first-person narrative and in the technique of creating a literary persona.[33] His tone, as we have seen, is conversational and playfully self-deprecating. In the very first issue after congratulating everyone on the New Year, he announces that he has always been sensible and polite, then admits at once that this is lie. Then at once he says he has told the lie as a moral lesson for his readers: "I am presenting you with this little moral on the magnificent occasion of the New Year." There are several examples in the journal of this special type of debunking satire. Čulkov likes to keep his readers guessing. In Week 3 he says: "By the way, don't believe everything I say, . . . I like lying and I am a great master at it; however, sometimes I tell the truth without wanting to . . .".

[33] It will be recalled that in Chapter I material from this journal was employed in an attempt to explain some of Čulkov's views, with the understanding that it is sometimes difficult to decide whether he is speaking for himself or simply assuming a mask.

I have noted earlier that Čulkov quotes Russian proverbs – this was not at all common in the printed literature of those times. The greatest concentration of proverbs in Čulkov's work occurs in *This and That*, particularly in the first few issues. A Russian scholar has counted fully seventy of these proverbs in the whole journal and notes that they have a national and popular character compared to those collected by the writer Bogdanovič at the request of Catherine a few years later. Many of the proverbs used by Čulkov are still in general use to this day.[34]

Čulkov's familiarity with such a large number of popular proverbs probably results in some measure from his modest social background, in which they would have been in common, everyday use. This would not have been the case in more aristocratic homes. It has also been suggested that Čulkov drew upon manuscript collections for some of these proverbs, and also for many of the short sketches and satirical anecdotes included at frequent intervals in the journal.[35] It is perhaps not too fanciful to suggest that Čulkov's fondness for such proverbs may also be partially due to the peculiar, often bipartite form which many of them take. They often consist of two more or less equal parts, with the second containing what we might think of as the 'punch line'. Let us take two examples from among the proverbs used by Čulkov: *Zerkalo ne vinovato, koli roža kriva* ("The mirror is not at fault, if your mug is crooked"), and *Don, Don, a doma lučše* ("Ah, the river Don, the Don, but home is better").[36] The undercutting quality of such proverbs must have appealed to Čulkov. An essential feature of Čulkov's use of the burlesque was his way of presenting material in an inflated style, and then in a direct and even vulgar style, thus pulling the rug out from under his reader's feet.

The undercutting quality is expressed in other ways which we met in the frame story of *The Mocker*: the use of a foreign word or simile, and then the vernacular Russian equivalent. A typical illustration of

[34] A. Zapadov, "Žurnal M. D. Čulkova *I to i së* i ego literaturnoe okruženie", in *XVIII Vek*, No. 2 (Moscow-Leningrad), p. 124. Zapadov mentions such proverbs as *Ispravit gorbatogo mogila* ("The grave will straighten out the hunchback"), *V lesu rubjat, a v mir ščepy letjat* (equivalent to: "You can't make an omelette without breaking eggs"), and *Um xorošo, a dva lučše togo* ("Two heads are better than one").

[35] Zapadov, *op. cit.*, p. 128.

[36] Readers of *Dead Souls* will recall that Gogol' used the first of these proverbs as the epigraph of his novel. We might note also that the incongruous contrast, more particularly that between vulgar detail and elegant and exquisite description, is quite common in Gogol'.

this occurs in Week 4 of the journal, in which Čulkov publishes a 'Letter from a traveling youth'. The young fellow complains that his father will give him not a penny although he is 'as wealthy as Croesus' and 'as miserly as Midas', or in Russian: 'as well off as an Olonec muzhik and as tightfisted as an Old Believer'.[37]

Of particular interest in this connection is one digression that takes place in an account of the guessing games played by young women and girls during Christmas time in Russia. Čulkov tells the story of a young man who dressed himself as a girl in order to be present at one of these guessing parties, when the young women sought to foretell whether they would soon be married and, if so, to what type of man. The story is told in the last November issue (Week 47), so it appeared at an appropriate time of year. Having told his readers of the young man's intentions, the narrator explains: "It was not Thetis who sent him to hide from the Trojan War, but he himself came to conquer the heart of one for whom he felt an inexplicable ardor." Two typical features are present here: Čulkov's mild mocking of the Classical reliance on divine interference in human affairs, and his use of burlesque in comparing the rather grubby plot of the young rogue to the events that took place before Troy according to the late Greek legend of Achilles, and indeed comparing the young man to the hero Achilles. This phrase takes on added significance once it is recalled that the same year 1769 saw the appearance of Čulkov's serious, not to say solemn, account of the pre-Trojan War Achilles legend. The reference here is of course to Thetis, the mother of the Greek hero, who disguised her son as a girl so that he would not take up arms and go to Troy to his death.

Čulkov himself could find little worthy of his admiration in the rival journals of 1769. His most extensive critique of them occurs in Week 24 (June), wherein he tells his readers that he had recently taken an old caftan inherited from his father to a French tailor to have it remodeled along more fashionable lines. The tailor confesses that he is puzzled by the great abundance of satirical journals: "At first I used to buy them, but I have stopped. They promised to be very useful, and yet when I looked them over, I found that all the writers of the journals

[37] Čulkov never missed a chance to satirize the Old Believers. See for example *Peresmešnik*, III, 220-221. Note also that the anti-Old Believer pamphlet *Žizn' nekotorogo muža* (Moscow, 1781) has been attributed to Čulkov, although there is still considerable doubt that he was the author.

keep saying the same things, only in different words; and it has been like this for sixth months now." [38]

The tailor can see little point in the constant quarreling among the rival journals.[39] He recommends that the new journals emulate '*The Bee* and the Academy publications', which in his opinion were far superior. *The Industrious Bee* was Sumarokov's journal which had been published ten years earlier, in 1759, the first privately owned journal in Russia. Čulkov is ashamed to tell the foreign tailor that he is the editor of *This and That*. The fictional episode with the tailor contains a seriously intended critique of the journals, including Čulkov's own. One is impressed when reading the journals by the similarity of the material and its monotony, and this may indeed indicate part of the reason for the failure of many of the journals to hold their readership and hence why they ceased publication so soon. Only the most persistent and industrious writers such as Čulkov and Nikolaj Novikov made repeated efforts to create a successful periodical.

Most scholars have agreed that both Čulkov journals lack the bitter social satire of Novikov's *Drone* and the satire of manners favored by the Empress Catherine in her *Hodgepodge*. Examples of both do occur in Čulkov's journals, but they are not characteristic of their contents as a whole. A. V. Zapadov writes of *This and That*: "In his journal Čulkov does not touch upon painful social problems. His polemical ardor is directed against literary foes. He rails against 'bad poets' and ridicules them, sometimes in a very crude manner." [40] Soviet scholars tend to regard Čulkov's journals, particularly *This and That*, as publications directed to the 'third estate'. For example, V. N. Putilov bases his discussion of both Čulkov's journals on the premise that in them he was attacking the nobility and attempting to serve the interests of merchants, civil servants, and others of the same social stratum.[41] At the same time Putilov quite rightly notes that Čulkov genuinely admired

[38] Only *Hodgepodge* and *This and That* had appeared in January, six months earlier.

[39] Novikov suggested much the same thing in his *Drone* (September 8), saying that one journal should preach virtue, another satirize vices, and a third "tell tales to amuse the simpleminded". The last remark was almost certainly aimed at Čulkov. Novikov's journals have been reprinted: *Satiričeskie žurnaly N. I. Novikova*, ed. P. N. Berkov (Moscow-Leningrad, 1951).

[40] A. V. Zapadov, "Žurnal M. D. Čulkova *I to i së* i ego literaturnoe okruženie", *XVIII Vek*, No. 2 (Moscow-Leningrad, 1940), p. 101).

[41] V. N. Putilov, "O žurnalax Čhulkova (*I to i së* i *Parnasskij ščepetil'nik*", *Učënye zapiski Leningradskogo gos. ped. instituta im. A. I. Gertena*, Vol. 29 (1940), 87-112.

certain aspects of Sumarokov's work and imitated his journal *The Industrious Bee*, and that Čulkov's criticism of Russian neo-classicism was not consistent.[42] A. V. Zapadov also argues that Čulkov was aiming to meet the needs of the middle classes, but does admit that it would be an exaggeration to portray him as the leader of a clearly defined anti-noble movement of the third estate.[43]

There is little evidence to support the assertion that Čulkov was aiming his journals at one particular group of readers or one particular social class, or that he was intending to voice the likes and dislikes of one particular group or class, although one suspects that the people who bought and read *This and That* would have been those without any foreign languages; upper class Russians generally read foreign works in the original and did not pay much attention to their own literature. One's impression is that by the variegated content of his material Čulkov sought to please and entertain as many people as possible so that they would buy his journal. While it is true that much space is given over to literary satire, the journal also contains many anecdotes, poems, and riddles. Several times in the journal Čulkov insists that he seeks only to entertain and to do this he includes verse and prose of many genres, both original and in translation. He also tries to inform and educate his readers, although he is never paternalistic. For example, he provides Russian explanations for a series of foreign words that he says are often inaccurately used by his compatriots, he explains the significance of Classical and some Slavic gods, and also discusses common Russian superstitions. In the last issue of *This and That* for December, 1769 (Weeks 51 and 52 combined) Čulkov bade farewell to his readers and gave his own estimate of what he had sought to do over the preceding year:

> I have cheered you with my prose; I have laughed at others, amused with fables, laughed artfully in epigrams, made time go faster for you with riddles, wept before you in elegies, and in every tale was ready to provide you with entertainment.

This gives an accurate indication of Čulkov's intentions and the contents of his first journal.

Several of the main features of Čulkov's prose discussed in previous chapters also find reflection in his second satirical journal *The Parnassian Trinket Dealer* (*Parnasskij ščepetil'nik*), a monthly that began to

[42] *Ibid.*, pp. 100 and 102.
[43] Zapadov, p. 95.

appear in May of 1770 and closed in December the same year.[44] Presumably Čulkov borrowed part of his title from that of a play by Vladimir Lukin, who had a few years earlier hit upon the Russian word *ščepetil'nik* as the best translation for the French *bijoutier*.[45] Since Čulkov began a second journal only a few months after the closing of his first journal *This and That* in December of 1769, one may well question the contention of some scholars that the satirical journals which sprang up so quickly following the appearance of Catherine's *Hodgepodge* ceased publication with similar rapidity as a direct result of government interference.

As the title *The Parnassian Trinket Dealer* itself suggests, the initial thrust of Čulkov's second journal was towards parodying and ridiculing 'bad poets', a theme that plays an important part in his first journal, particularly in his three burlesque narrative poems which have just been discussed. This theme in fact runs through much of Čulkov's work, both prose and verse. Such satires and parodies were a common feature of French seventeenth-century classicism and of Russian eighteenth-century neo-classicism, especially in the works of Sumarokov. Čulkov uses it several times in *The Mocker*, for example, in the frame story and in the tale narrated by the monk, "The Tale of the Origin of the Taffeta Beauty Spot". At one point in the story the student Neox manages to change clothes with a peasant killed in a brawl and so escapes the priests who are seeking him for the attempted murder of Vladimira's father. Neox sets out for Vineta and sends word to Vladimira in Novgorod to join him there. She is overjoyed to hear from him at last and at once gets ready to leave. Her steward is named Kuromša, a man as short as a dwarf, eighty-four years old, who is passionately in love with Vladimira's maid, a girl of fifteen.[46] He is a grotesque figure: "What

[44] *Parnasskij ščepetil'nik* (St. Petersburg, 1770). This journal has numbered pages and individual sections are given Roman numerals which continue consecutively until the end of the year. The Library of Congress has a copy of the issues from May to September.

[45] Lukin's play *Ščepetil'nik* was an adaptation of a French translation of *The Toyshop* by Robert Dodsley, entitled *Boutique de bijoutier*. See: *Russkaja komedija i komičeskaja opera XVIII veka*, ed. P. N. Berkov (Moscow-Leningrad, 1950), p. 683. A text of Lukin's play is given in this work.

[46] Čulkov was fond of making fun of short men who were also poets, and no doubt the fact that Popov, his friend and literary collaborator, was short had something to do with this (Čulkov himself was reputed to have been of above average height). However, we shall see in the next chapter that Paul Scarron's novel *Le roman comique* had a great influence on Čulkov, and one of the characters in this novel is Ragotin, who is a figure of fun, very short, an execrable poet, and in love with a young girl.

nature had taken from his stature, it had put back in his nose." His nose is huge, red, crooked, and spread across his face, so that he has trouble seeing over or around it. Kuromša is heartbroken when he is obliged to stay behind while his beloved accompanies her mistress to Vineta to rejoin Neox. He has literary pretensions and has been reworking the migratory tale "Prince Bova" into an heroic poem for about thirty years. Now, in this moment of anguish he turns to the composition of an elegy on the departure of his beloved. This elegy, the 'saddest type of poem', he is quoted in full. It is a parody, containing many exclamations such as 'alack!', 'woe!', and 'alas!', and it is very repetitious. One line reads: "Farewell, farewell, farewell, and again I say, farewell." [47]

The narrator then steps forward to condemn the elegy and the many rhymers and poetasters of his day who are overpraised by the ladies, the objects of their verses: "This work has been quoted here in order to put to shame those insensitive poets who in reading their works see nothing wrong with them and declare that their useless lines are the flower of poetry." [48]

It is, therefore, no surprise to find Čulkov turning to this theme once again in his second journal in 1770. He begins his opening issue of *The Parnassian Trinket Dealer* in much the same mood as he had left his readers at the end of the previous year. He declines with exaggerated modesty the honorable title of author, but confesses that he still has the urge to write.[49] Čulkov also admits that he has been attacking a number of poets, referring presumably to his burlesque poems in *This and That*, and then adds a brief footnote:

What I say has nothing to do with learned people who have been and are to this day famous for their achievements here and throughout Russia; it refers directly to very poorly educated scribblers of poetry. I will not undertake to shower praise on Mr. Sumarokov further, nor upon the late Lomonosov, knowing that they are both deserving of great praise. But which of them has done the greater good to the country and earned the greater fame – that is something I will leave to the judgment of people far more enlightened than I am.[50]

[47] *Peresmešnik, ili Slavenskie skazki*, 3d. ed. (Moscow, 1789), Part IV, p. 184. Parts III and IV of *Peresmešnik* were first published in 1768. The parodical elegy was also printed in the journal *I to i së* (Week 7).
[48] *Ibid.*, IV, 185.
[49] Čulkov here seems to be referring to his complaints about the lot of the writer in Week 48 of *I to i së* (see Chapter I, p. 29).
[50] *Parnasskij ščepetil'nik*, I, 4. In the discussion that follows reference will be made in the text by Roman and Arabic numerals, indicating section and page of the journal.

At its face value this statement is a disavowal on Čulkov's part of any intention to satirize or parody the work of Sumarokov and Lomonosov. Safeguarding himself still further, Čulkov modestly and perhaps with tongue in cheek declines to say which of the two major Russian poets of the time he prefers, even though he has little to lose since one of them is already dead. The fact of the matter is, as we have seen, that Čulkov did parody Lomonosov and to a lesser extent Sumarokov in his burlesque poems. That he felt it necessary to make his intentions clear suggests he had indeed given offense to some people, notably Sumarokov himself. It is likely that Čulkov had offended Sumarokov by making fun of some of his lines and also by parodying Vasilij Majkov, who was one of Sumarokov's leading disciples.

Although their literary interests and practice by no means coincided, Čulkov and Sumarokov had previously been on friendly terms, at least professionally. They may well have met at first through Čulkov's association with the court theater in St. Petersburg. Čulkov praised Sumarokov's journal *The Industrious Bee* and even imitated its format in his own journal *This and That*, and joined in attacking Fëdor Èmin, one of Sumarokov's *bêtes noirs*. It has been noted that Sumarokov contributed to two February issues of Čulkov's first journal before he left St. Petersburg to settle in Moscow. We can assume, therefore, that Čulkov had badly miscalculated in his burlesque poems. Sumarokov satirized him in one of his fables entitled "The Judgment of Paris" ("Parisov sud").[51]

Čulkov further aggravated matters in 1770 by taking it upon himself to make some alterations in poems written by Sumarokov which he included in the first volume of his *Collection of Various Songs*. In the preface to his new tragedy *The False Dimitrij* (*Dimitrij samozvanec,* 1771), which consists of a tirade against the decline of Russian letters brought about by the entrance of commoners upon the literary scene, Sumarokov remarked: "It is unseemly for a lackey, even a court lackey, to ruin, print, and sell my songs without my permission." Although Čulkov was not mentioned by name, anyone in the literary circles of the time must have understood who was meant. This naturally marked an open break between the two men.

In his journal *The Parnassian Trinket Dealer*, Čulkov continued to

[51] *A. P. Sumarokov: Izbrannye proizvedenija*, 2nd ed. (Leningrad, 1957), p. 227. Scholars have been unable to date the fable, but it could not have been written earlier than the beginning of 1770.

develop his theme of the overcrowded Parnassus and the necessity for thinning out the ranks of poetasters, but he took care not to make references to Sumarokov, Lomonosov, or Vasilij Majkov. According to Čulkov, there were some one hundred thousand poets on Parnassus, and so Apollo with the agreement of the Muses had decided to sell off some of them, send some as translators and writers of lengthy exhortations (*racei*) and eulogies (*kanty*) to distant provincial towns, and others as priests to equally remote villages (I, 5, May). Apollo appoints Čulkov the auctioneer. Čulkov accepts the appointment and announces that he will auction authors, also the works of good authors (and his own). He promises his readers that he will seek to avoid offending 'delicate ears' and will not send himself self-congratulatory letters (I, 10); was this another jibe at Catherine's journal?

He then proceeds to describe the first poet to be auctioned in a section entitled "Dramatic Poet For Sale" (II, 12, May). Čulkov goes into some detail about his character and the style of his works. The 'dramatic poet' writes poems composed only of monosyllables with the result that his lines are "neither witty nor artful (*zamyslovatyj*), but just like Italian notes played on a Russian *gudok*" (a three-stringed instrument). The poet, like most of those lampooned by Čulkov, is conceited and behaves rather oddly: "He often strides along streets simply in order to correct the grammatical mistakes made by peasants, and struggles with them defending wisdom with the palm of his hand and his fists." He always walks with his head bowed, deep in thought. Once he walked right into a lamppost in the street and knocked his head quite a blow (II, 13). His works are listed for the benefit of prospective buyers:

1. "The Abode of Lawlessness," in verse.
2. "Harmful Fashion," in verse.
3. "Deceit," in blank verse.
4. "Bad Conversations," in prose.
5. "Rubbish of All Sorts," in prose.
6. "On My Own Want of Wit," in verse and prose (II, 14).

Čulkov offers to sell the poet and his works together for the sum of one ruble and eight grivna.

There have been attempts to match Čulkov's 'dramatic poet' with one of his well-known contemporaries. However, the poet's characteristics and works seem to have little to do with any particular writer, and P. N. Berkov is doubtless correct in suggesting that Čulkov's portrait will not match any of his contemporaries because it is a composite portrait in which Čulkov satirizes several men, not just one.[52] The work in blank verse may refer to Mixail Xeraskov, for he had indeed experimented in this manner a few years earlier. Berkov has discovered a poem written in words of one syllable by A. A. Rževskij in the journal *Useful Enjoyment* (*Poleznoe uveselenie*), and also notes that Vladimir Lukin was in the habit of walking with his head bowed and once bumped into a street light: this incident seems to have created a good deal of amusement and has thus been recorded for posterity.[53]

The second author to be auctioned is a lyric poet, who wears a four-cornered hat and again suffers from an inflated opinion of his own importance: "As though he were an ancient law-giver, he expects people to raise a statue to him, not made of vulgar stone, but of the marble that has been found in the lakes nearby; and he wants his verses to be preserved in special golden vessels" (III, 15). He sells serfs in order to get ready cash, and has a weakness for imported French confectionary. Čulkov is unable to list his works since none is known: they are still housed in an obscure provincial library. He offers to give the poet away for nothing. There is very little to go on here, and it seems quite likely that this is again a composite portrait.

Čulkov then sets out to summon other poets for auction. In various issues of his journal up to and including the issue for July Čulkov continued to return to this theme of auctioning poets, but one notes that he begins to get a little repetitious. Once again we find him making fun of an old and very short poet who is in love with a young woman (twice as tall as he is and twice as intelligent). Another poet has a grandfather who is 'a pillar of the Old Believers'; the description of this unpleasant character is almost identical with that in *The Mocker* (Part III, 219-221). This sort of material becomes monotonous, and the references to the various foibles of the poets more and more esoteric. The identification of Čulkov's possible targets becomes the only point of any interest; the literary aspects of his satire are minimal.

At the beginning of the issue for July Čulkov says that news of his intention to auction poets and their works has apparently had no effect upon them; they continue to write on political and juridical matters and complain that Čulkov's work is not improving the manners and morals of *petits-maîtres* (XIII, 99). As in the previous year in his journal *This*

[52] P. N. Berkov, *Istorija russkoj žurnalistiki XVIII veka* (Moscow-Leningrad, 1952), p. 267.
[53] Berkov, *op. cit.*, p. 268.

and That, Čulkov refuses to engage in the type of satire advocated by either Catherine or Nikolaj Novikov. He declares that he prefers to direct his satire only at poets: "I want to be modest and I shall speak of those slanderous poets who inhumanely prey upon virtuous and beautiful women, so that the whole of the fair sex will be on my side" (XIII, 100).

In this same section of the July issue of the journal we find Čulkov returning to one of his favorite topics, the purposes and effects of literature. Čulkov repeats his belief, which he had stated on a number of occasions in *The Mocker*, that literature cannot reform or improve, and he even seems to suggest that this is not the purpose of literature at all. In *The Mocker* he had spoken in terms of the prose genres, but he now states his view with regard to the theater, taking as an example a play by Vladimir Lukin:

> The spendthrift always laughs at the comedy *The Spendthrift*, and the vain man who has no merits or virtues except his pedigree is delighted when he sees someone like himself presented on the stage. The Francophile Russian roars with laughter at the spectacle of a Russian who has newly returned from France having forgotten his own language and who disdains the manners of his own country. In just the same way the feeble-minded versifier smiles as he reads this.... (XIII, 101).

The final self-mocking phrase is very typical of Čulkov's narrative manner, that part of it which we have called the 'undercutting' technique. Čulkov ends by admitting that he knows his own satires against bad poets will have no effect whatsoever. We might note that, holding the views he did, Čulkov ought to have stayed away from satire completely.

There is a brief anecdote told about one of the unfortunate poets being hounded by the auctioneer which in certain aspects suggests the developing critical attitude of Čulkov towards the magical transformations that figure so largely in Ladon's narrative in *The Mocker*. However, it does not represent any substantial advance on the self-parody we find in some of the young monk's tales. Having been rejected by a young woman, the poet writes a vicious satire against the woman 'in the manner of Juvenal'. The woman's lover, a young merchant, gathers together some of his friends and they manage to get the poet drunk, then lay him unconscious in a grave surrounded by lights. When he awakens from his drunken stupor he believes he must be in hell. A man dressed as a bear approaches the frightened poet and tells him that he is now in a kingdom controlled by a great sorceress Kanidija, who is about two thousand years old and has fallen madly in love with him.[54] He warns the poet that he had better respond to the ancient woman's caresses, or else she will turn him into a bear or a lion. Soon the old hag arrives and the 'unfortunate bard' (*neščastnyj piit*) is obliged to pretend he is in love with her (XIV, 113). At this point six 'devils' arrive and give the poet a thorough thrashing, put him in a sack with only his head visible and abandon him. Like some episodes in the monk's tales this story readers like a satirical commentary on certain parts of Ladon's narrative in *The Mocker*. One notes that all the magical elements – the sorceress, the talking bear, the threatened transformation, the devils – all have their rational explanation as part of an elaborate hoax played upon the poet. The realistic element in the story is, however, fairly small and the story could well be set in the same 'misty Varangian times' as the monk's longest tale about the taffeta beauty spot.

Much of the material in *The Parnassian Trinket Dealer* is of a most humdrum nature. Gradually the journal began to be taken up with more and more translated material, including parts of relatively obscure works such as Agrippa von Nettesheim's *De Incertitudine et Vanitate Scientiarum*, which appeared originally in 1531. The last four issues of the journal for September through December are almost overwhelmed with translations and material of very little interest, as can be seen from the outline of contents given by Neustroev.[55] Clearly Čulkov was simply marking time during the last four months of the year. He was running out of steam and one is not surprised that he closed the journal at the end of 1770. He was probably more concerned with the preparation for publication of his *Collection of Various Songs*.

[54] The old hag Canidia ocurs in the works of Horace, for example in *Satires*, I. 8 and in *Epodes* 3, 5 and 17. Latin literature was familiar to Čulkov from his studies at the Gymnasium of Moscow University. In this connection see Wolfgang Busch, *Horaz in Russland* (Munich, 1964).

[55] *Istoričeskoe rozyskanie o russkix povremennyx izdanijax i sbornikax za 1703-1802 gg.* (St. Petersburg, 1874), pp. 159-161.

IV

THE RHETORIC OF FICTION: USES AND LIMITATIONS

While the influences on Čulkov's work were multifarious and often difficult to trace, the most important was probably that of the French seventeenth-century anti-romance, and in particular Paul Scarron's *Le roman comique*. That he was so profoundly influenced by a French author who wrote in the first half of the seventeenth century illustrates the wide range of influences at work during the reign of Catherine II, and incidentally, the cultural time lag under which Russian writers of the period were operating. Scarron seems to have been quite unknown in Russia until one hundred years after his death in 1660. His novel did not appear in Russian translation until 1763, by which time he had been almost totally forgotten in his own country.[1]

To demonstrate the direct influence of Scarron upon Čulkov one has only to turn to the beginning of *The Mocker*. At the end of the first chapter of the frame story the narrator says of his characters: "While they begin eating, I will think about the organization of my second chapter."[2] The parallel between this and the ending of Scarron's opening chapter is obvious. In *Le roman comique* the animals pulling the cart that holds the comedy actors and their belongings are given something to eat and Scarron remarks: "Cependant que ses bestes mangèrent, l'Auteur se reposa quelque temps et se mit à songer à ce qu'il diroit dans le second Chapitre."[3]

Further evidence of Scarron's influence is provided by the frame

[1] *Šutlivaja povest'*, Parts I and II (St. Petersburg, 1763). This translation was made by Vasilij Teplov from a German version, not the original French. Šklovskij was the first to remark upon Scarron's influence on Čulkov, in his monograph, *Čulkov i Levšin* (Leningrad, 1933).

[2] *Russkaja proza XVIII veka*, I (Moscow-Leningrad, 1950), 96. One finds many examples of this sort of thing in Gogol'. At one point in *Mërtvye duši* he announces that he will take advantage of a character falling asleep to tell his life story.

[3] Paul Scarron, *Le Romant Comique*, Texte établi et présenté par Henri Bénac, I (Paris, 1951), 95.

story's chapter headings, which are often deliberately comic. For example, Chapter Ten is headed: "If you read it, you will know what is in it without any title." In Scarron's novel Chapter Five is entitled: "Qui ne contient pas grand'chose" and Chapter Eleven: "Qui contient ce que vous verrez, si vous prenez la peine de le lire." As if to confirm these indications of direct influence Čulkov refers to one of the characters in the frame story, Balaban, as 'a nephew of Scarron's late comedy actor Zlobin'. Zlobin is the Russian name taken by calque from La Rancune, one of the chief characters in *Le roman comique*. Čulkov may indeed have considered himself a sort of Russian Scarron, if we can put trust in a verse epigram that was directed against him in 1769 by his arch-enemy in literary matters, Fëdor Èmin.[4] Èmin's epigram takes the form of a 'Riddle' and a 'Solution' and in one couplet he poses the question: "Who has written tales about everything under the sun / And believes that he is another Scarron?"[5] So there is ample evidence for believing that Čulkov had read and admired Scarron, and was even attempting to follow in his footsteps. Just as Scarron had satirized and parodied the contemporary heroic or 'précieux' novel *Le Grand Cyrus* by Madeleine de Scudéry, so we see Čulkov in his turn parodying the almost equally lengthy and involved novels of Èmin, which follow quite closely in the same tradition. And yet the reader of Ladon's narrative in *The Mocker* must find it striking that Čulkov was really parodying himself, or rather that there is a dialectic at work, a dialectic of thesis and antithesis between the narratives of Ladon and the young monk. Doubtless this element of self-parody in *The Mocker* derives largely from the instability of the traditions of narrative prose in Russia at this time. Čulkov was clearly experimenting with the traditions and themes available, and investigating their possibilities.

Čulkov's situation as a writer of prose fiction, and particularly of anti-romance, in a predominantly neo-classical environment was remarkably similar to that of Scarron a century before. One might argue that Scarron did not plant the seed, but at least he may be said to have cultivated it and directed its growth. He had a vital influence both on the Russian writer's selection and treatment of material and also on narrative technique. The two are of course inter-related, but we can

[4] This epigram appeared in Nikolaj Novikov's journal *Truten'* (List XIV, July 28, 1769) and was a reply to an attack by Čulkov in *I to i së* upon the journals of both Èmin (*Adskaja počta*) and Novikov.

[5] "Kto v skazkax napisal sorok da voron / I vzdumal o sebe, čto budto on Skarron?" Tales about "magpies and crows" (*sorok da voron*) would mean tales about trivial things, fairy tales of no importance.

discuss them here separately under the headings of burlesque and the self-conscious narrator.

Paul Scarron, the author of *Le roman comique*, is equally well-known for his travesty of Vergil's *Aeneid*, and it was the burlesque references to Classical mythology in Scarron's novel that seem most to have attracted Čulkov's attention. He includes seriously intended periphrastic descriptions of dawn and dusk in Ladon's narrative, but in the frame story and in the monk's tales we find parodies of such Classical periphrases. Here is an example: "When the sun was beginning to nod and his steeds were pretty well exhausted and wanted something to eat, then in the house servants were ordered to lay the table." [6] The reader is reminded of the famous opening lines of *Le roman comique*:

Le soleil avoit achevé plus de la moitié de sa course et son char, ayant attrappé le penchant du monde, rouloit plus viste qu'il ne vouloit. Si les chevaux eussent voulu profiter de la pente du chemin, ils eussent achevé ce qui restoit du jour en moins d'un demy-quart d'heure: Mais, au lieu de tirer de toute leur force, ils ne s'amusoient qu'à faire des courbettes, respirant un air marin qui les faisoit hannir et les advertissoit que la mer estoit proche, ou l'on dit que leur Maistre se couche toutes les nuits. Pour parler plus humainement et plus intelligiblement, il estoit entre cinq et six quand une charette entra dans les Halles du Mans.

In the frame story the monk uses another similarly parodical phrase: "The sun's steeds had already passed the Eastern winds, which emerged with them at the same time and from the same place, while ours carried us out of the forest." [7]

Like Scarron, Čulkov also degrades the mythological gods, both Classical and Slavic, which he had employed in a traditionally serious manner in Ladon's narrative. Thus Bacchus appears in a rather vulgar tale told in the frame story.[8] But generally speaking, in his prose Čulkov does not use the degrading burlesque nearly as much as Scarron.

Burlesque is used by Čulkov throughout the frame story and the tales narrated by the young monk, but most frequently in the monk's longest tale, "The Tale of the Origin of the Taffeta Beauty Spot". This tale, which is begun in the middle of the third part (or volume) of *The Mocker* and completed in the fifth, is supposedly set in the same place and time as Ladon's narrative, for we find the same city of Vineta mentioned, as well as the pagan temples. As the title suggests, the tale

[6] *Russkaja proza XVIII veka*, p. 106.
[7] *Ibid.*, p. 117.
[8] *Ibid.*, p. 99.

purports to tell how beauty spots, or rather their taffeta variety, came to be invented. Although we cannot be sure whether Čulkov was directly familiar with them (perhaps in French translation?), there were in England in the first half of the eighteenth century a great many mock-heroic or high burlesque poems which professed to relate the origin of such objects of the fashionable lady's toilet and boudoir as the beauty spot. The best-known example of such poems is probably "The Fan" (1714) written by John Gay. Čulkov's tale in prose clearly belongs to this same tradition, even if we cannot be sure how he came to it.

What one notes particularly about Čulkov's tale is that he prefers to write in prose, not verse. Furthermore, he has combined this tradition with elements of the picaresque, so that the larger part of the tale concerns the adventures of the rogue Neox, a penniless student at the University of Novgorod! During the course of the tale Neox makes the acquaintance of the daughter of the high priest at the temple of Černobog ('Black God') in Novgorod, attempts to kill the girl's father for his money (at her suggestion), escapes from prison, travels to the city of Vineta, becomes the gigolo of the wife of a merchant, then secretary to an influential official, and finally makes a very successful marriage to the daughter of a powerful courtier and even becomes an intimate friend of the local ruler or king.

The most obvious examples of burlesque occur in brief phrases, such as the reference to a footman bearing a note as 'Mercury'.[9] Čulkov is quite fond of using the god Mercury in this way. Sometimes he adds oxymoron to the incongruous burlesque contrast, as when he refers to the cuckolded merchant as 'this grey and toothless Mercury'.[10] Both these examples are taken from "The Tale of the Origin of the Taffeta Beauty Spot", but many others may be found in the frame story.

A more extended instance of burlesque occurs in this same tale about the taffeta beauty spot which is narrated by the monk. During the course of his adventures the young student Neox comes across a deserted peasant hut. He goes in and falls asleep on the sleeping berth (*polati*) near the ceiling. Later he is awakened by the sounds of a man and woman talking excitedly. When he tries to move over in order to

[9] *Peresmešnik*, III, 168. A messenger gives Neox a billet-doux from a young lady. The narrator calls the man "a descendant of the late Mercury, namely a footman" (*naslednik pokojnogo Merkurija, a imenno, skoroxod*).

[10] *Ibid.*, IV, 238. Neox manages to trick the merchant into believing that the high priest and a very respectable noblewoman are having an affair and persuades him to act as their go-between.

see who they are, he falls down bringing the planks of wood down with him. The narrator comments:

> The destruction of the walls of Troy did not make as much noise as the planks did thundering down to the ground. The unfortunate Vulcan, whom Jupiter had cast down from the sky onto an island, broke his leg; but our Vulcan in falling down from the sleeping berth onto the floor remained safe and sound, except that he struck the back of his head somewhat, which made his ears ring and stars appear before his eyes.[11]

This is a good illustration of the high burlesque, the mock portrayal of a rather humdrum and even farcical incident in terms of lofty Classical mythology.

We find the history of the Trojan War being used in an equally extended burlesque reference in another tale narrated by the monk, which is entitled "The Miser and the Thief" ("Skupoj i vor"). The son of a miserly landowner near Moscow falls in love and desperately needs money. With the help of his servant he attempts to dig a tunnel from the garden in order to get access to his father's fortune, which is prudently kept under lock and key in the cellar of the house. A series of farcical events follows, during which the father dies, is buried, the joyful son gives a lavish funeral repast, and then the father comes back to life again when one of his servants digs up his body to try to steal his clothes. The son flees, with his irate and resurrected father in hot pursuit, but both are shot by an officer still drunk from the funeral repast. In describing the commotion caused by the old man's resurrection the narrator says:

> There was more panic in the house than at the destruction of the city of Troy. The Trojans were defeated in their city, but here all the peasants ran for about four days through the woods, and some of them were so terrified that they wanted to become hermits.[12]

It should be obvious from these examples that the high burlesque involves the use of material from Classical literature and mythology, and that this material is introduced in similes and comparisons. The simile

[11] *Peresmešnik*, IV, 192. The use of the walls of Troy in high burlesque is specifically suggested by Sumarokov in his epistle from which I have already quoted at the beginning of the previous chapter. I might note in passing that many Russians were introduced to the Trojan War not by Homer, but by Guido delle Colonne, whose thirteenth-century *Historia Destructionis Troiae* was first translated into Russian in 1745: *Istorija o razoveni i Troi*. This work is mentioned by Čulkov in *The Mocker*. Guido's history is a prose version of the *Roman de Troie* by Benoît de Sainte-Maure.

[12] *Russkaja proza XVIII veka*, p. 138.

used in this way is of course not typical in the traditional burlesque, whether high or low. However, it must be remembered that Čulkov's tales and stories are not burlesque works in their entirety. Consequently, he was operating outside the burlesque and was obliged to employ the simile or comparison as a device to create the incongruous contrast that he desired.

The monk's longest tale opens with the narrator grumbling good-naturedly about scholars who waste their time studying useless subjects, instead of those that are of especial interest to men and women in fashionable high society who want to learn about fine clothes and things of that sort. The narrator selects the beauty spot as an example of what he has in mind:

> I think that Vergil and Homer, for all their great wisdom, are not worth even the little finger of that great man who composed the register of beauty spots, so useful to fashionable society. And as for Aesop, with all his fables he is not even fit to be a coachman. Aesop gave tongue and voice only to wild animals, cattle, birds, and snakes; but this unparalleled man also opened the mouth of an inanimate object – fops and coquettes understand it.[13]

It is true that we do not have an example of the burlesque with incongruous mythological references, but the same principle of incongruity is at work. The principle of the burlesque is applied, but it is used to degrade the Classical authors, or rather to poke fun at the fops and coquettes, whose spokesman the narrator is at this point.

Very much the same may be said of the numerous references to the figures of Classical mythology which occur in this tale, even when the burlesque element is not paramount. Neox suddenly receives a sum of money from an aunt and the narrator suggests in an aside that some god must have whispered in the aunt's ear that she should send Neox the money. Neox gathers together four of his fellow students for a tremendous feast at which five young and pliable ladies are present. They all enjoy themselves far into the night and then the narrator coyly remarks that he will say no more: "let us allow Venus to finish what Bacchus has begun".[14] Having lavished all his wealth on this party, Neox is left penniless, but once again fortune smiles upon him, this time in the form of Vladimira, the rich and willful young daughter of the high priest of the temple of Černobog. Vladimira has Neox brought to her room for a rendezvous and rewards him with money and jewels, which he at once spends on another gargantuan banquet. The author

[13] *Peresmešnik*, III, 151.
[14] *Ibid.*, 164.

interrupts his description of the rather unheroic events taking place at the party to note that Neox 'sacrificed equally to both Aphrodite and Minerva'.[15]

The burlesque concept, whether Čulkov obtained it from Sumarokov or Scarron (surely the latter's examples were more influential), lies at the heart of the basic feature of Čulkov's style: a series of incongruous contrasts. He develops the concept beyond the straightforward burlesque. The essential feature of Čulkov's method, as can be seen more clearly from some of the illustrations that follow, is his way of presenting the material in a high style and then as it were pulling the rug from under his reader's feet by calling a spade a spade.

There are of course frequent occurrences of burlesque elsewhere in the tales narrated by the monk and also in the frame story. The nephew of the colonel in the frame story who acts as Ladon's protector is named Balaban; he is a wealthy ignoramus, likened to an animal in his behavior – a worthy successor to Mitrofan in Fonvizin's comedy *The Minor* (*Nedorosl'*).[16] Balaban mistakes a tobacco pouch for bagpipes and chokes on the contents. Later in the frame story Balaban falls in love and the narrator supplies us with this elaborate explanation for the appearance of this emotion: "At the beginning of the autumn Venus determined to present in our house a traveling comedy, or more simply a farce (*igrišče*), and for this purpose she sent her son to visit us."[17] Balaban decides to send the object of his passions some love poems, which he copies out of a book; they are in fact satires.

These examples tend to show that while burlesque may be perfectly natural and legitimate in certain types of verse, specifically as a weapon for satire and parody, its presence in prose fiction can be a limiting factor and date a work rather badly. One notes also that Čulkov demonstrates a marked preference for the high burlesque, which is employed when the subject-matter is 'low', that is, taken from everyday Russian life. It is interesting to recall a remark made by one of the leading Soviet Russian scholars of eighteenth-century Russian literature, Grigorij Gukovskij. He noted that both Sumarokov and Fonvizin, as

[15] *Ibid.*, 192.

[16] The word "balaban" was originally a Turkic borrowing, already widespread some time before this use by Čulkov. It meant "dolt" or "braggard"; the name suits Balaban.

[17] *Russkaja proza XVIII veka*, I, p. 123. The word *igrišče* was evidently a technical term used in the theater and would have been known to Čulkov from his own personal experience. The translation of Christoph Cellarius' lexicon *Kratkoj latinskoj leksikon s rossijskim i nemeckim perevodom* (St. Petersburg, 1768) has an entry "Ludi, pozorišče, igrišče, Schauspiele."

representatives of Russian neo-classicism, posited an ideal reality to which they contrasted the vulgar reality they saw around them. These men, and others of the same literary persuasion at that time, condemned the vulgar reality, since they regarded it as 'irrational'. Their reaction was naturally either to ignore it or to attempt to improve it. If they adopted the latter course, the only weapon at their disposal was satire. Gukovskij comments:

"Positive" heroes and themes are given in the abstract manner; the negative in their negative (for the Classicist) real concreteness. Sumarokov felt hostility towards this concrete reality and portrayed it in an attempt to fight against it. So it was that in Russian Classicism the facts of concrete reality, of real life, appeared as a theme for satire, accompanied by the author's clearly defined attitude of censorship and disapproval. Sumarokov's fables, satires, later comedies, and articles are quite characteristic in this connection.[18]

In his works which we have discussed thus far Čulkov fits fairly well into this pattern. On the one hand he wrote about idealized heroes and heroines in an abstract manner; the characters in Ladon's narrative are all nobly born and they all behave nobly (except of course for the villain Askalon) – they represent human perfection in their faithfulness, devotion, and courage. And on the other hand Čulkov wrote about amoral and immoral rogues in a burlesque and satirical manner. So that the subject matter, the characters, and the treatment accorded them differ in the two types of narrative. Čulkov's attitude towards concrete Russian reality was not quite the same as that held by Sumarokov, but his treatment of the material from it clearly was influenced by the Russian neo-classical *Weltanschauung*, which Gukovskij has tried to define. Gukovskij goes on to point out that Fonvizin shared the views embraced by Sumarokov, but that he was able to create a handful of 'living' characters in his two comedies. Čulkov too succeeded in creating a handful of interesting and lively characters, but none who really 'come to life', certainly not in the works we have discussed thus far.

For a neo-classical tragedian with a sense of grandeur and psychological finesse the concept of an ideal reality, of *la belle nature*, and the satirical attitude towards contemporary reality would not become seriously inhibiting factors. However, for a prose writer like Čulkov

[18] Gr. Gukovskij, *Očerki po istorii russkoj literatury i obščestvennoj mysli XVIII veka* (Leningrad, 1938), p. 186. Much the same point about the effects of the neo-classical outlook on contemporary reality and the positing of an ideal reality which is treated idealistically is made in Erich Auerbach, *Mimesis* (Princeton, 1953). See: Chapter 15, "The Faux Dévot".

with his quite different talents, they most certainly did. Ladon's narrative is rather too obviously derivative, and Čulkov was as little at home in the idealistic manner as he would have been in the verse genres he parodied in his burlesque poems. He was obliged to hold back from commenting on the action and found it hard to maintain the appropriate solemn tone throughout the work.

The monk's tales are much more successful and illustrate the features of Čulkov's natural narrative manner. And yet one is bound to admit that, as in Scarron's travesty of the *Aeneid* and to a lesser extent in his *Roman comique*, the burlesque can soon become monotonous. The endless references to mythological figures are very tiresome and date his works. Nowadays we find it difficult to appreciate the traditional Classical burlesque.[19] Much the same may be said about the constant bantering tone of Čulkov's narrator. There is the ever-present danger that the reader will tire of the unaltered mocking tone. Such a rogue's gallery presents a picture of life which is just as one-sided and unreal as that presented in Ladon's narrative. As has been justly remarked, the works of Sorel and Scarron frequently threaten to become as far removed from reality as the idealistic 'romances' of such French authors as Honoré d'Urfé and Madeleine de Scudéry, whom they sought to parody and ridicule. In engaging in parody, both of others and partly of himself, Čulkov ran the risk of frittering away his talent on reacting to works instead of creating something new of his own. His self-parodies are an essential part of his early work, because they provide us with clear evidence of his growing critical attitude towards one of the narrative prose traditions that was popular at the time, and consequently they illustrate his literary development. However, a literary apprenticeship cannot last forever.

Čulkov's reading of Scarron's novel not only had an effect on his attitude toward and treatment of his material, but also on his method of narration, which is explicitly rhetorical. We have already noted that asides and digressions play a much more important part in those portions of *The Mocker* narrated by the young monk. These asides include some which are fairly routine, for example those directed against *petits-maîtres* and coquettes. In "The Tale of the Origin of the Taffeta Beauty Spot" the narrator stops to digress on this subject after Neox has flattered a woman by saying he was dazzled by her beauty: "It is well

[19] I would exclude from these remarks Čulkov's extension of the burlesque principle and his quite imaginative use of other than mythological methods of incongruous contrast.

known that women receive such speeches with the greatest pleasure and joy, and they find them pleasanter than rebukes. Nowadays, whoever possesses the gift of pleasing a fashionable coquette will without doubt find opened to him the numberless doors of the temple of Venus."[20] There is nothing very novel about this sort of aside. Of greater interest are digressions made by what is known as the self-conscious narrator, who makes no attempt to withdraw from the action or to pretend that his narrative is anything more than his own invention.[21] This rhetorical manner was widespread in the eighteenth century throughout Europe and later came to be employed to great effect by Puškin, notably in *Eugene Onegin*, and by Gogol'.

This kind of digression calls attention to the mechanics and techniques of narration. *Tristram Shandy*, which appeared almost exactly at the same time as *The Mocker*, is regarded as the high point of this device.[22] The Russian Formalist critics paid particular attention to this technique of narration, which they called 'laying bare the device' (*obnaženie priëma*).[23] Once again, as with Čulkov's use of the burlesque, it seems obvious that the initial stimulus for his rhetorical method of narrating came from *Le roman comique*. We have already quoted at the beginning of this chapter a number of examples of parallel phrases from Scarron's novel and *The Mocker*, including one in which Ladon as narrator of the frame story announces that he will begin thinking about what to write in the following chapter while his characters are busy eating. Čulkov seems to have been particularly taken by the method Scarron often used to bring his chapters to a close. At the end of Chapter Six in the frame story he has Ladon say: "However my joy is not so powerful as sleep, which is already beginning to close my eyes

[20] *Peresmešnik*, III, 185.

[21] For a discussion of the self-conscious narrator in Western European fiction see: Wayne C. Booth, *The Rhetoric of Fiction* (Chicago, 1961). Čulkov's use of the self-conscious narrator differentiates him from the anonymous authors of the Russian seventeenth-century manuscript satires who, as V. P. Adrianova-Peretc points out, "never engage in a direct dialogue with the reader". See: *Russkaja demokratičeskaja satira XVII veka* (Moscow-Leningrad, 1954), p. 171.

[22] The serialized publication of Sterne's novel in fact came to an end in 1767. Sterne himself probably did not take the technique directly from Scarron. Booth remarks that "in general Scarron only adumbrates devices that Sterne could have learned much more about from later writers". See Booth's article "The Self-Conscious Narrator in Comic Fiction before *Tristram Shandy*", *PMLA*, LXVII (March 1952), 170.

[23] Šklovskij is the author of the major study of "laying bare the device": "Parodijnyj roman. *Tristram Šendi* Sterna", in his book *O teorii prozy* (Moscow-Leningrad, 1925), pp. 139-161. He does not discuss Čulkov's use of the device either in this article or in his *Čulkov i Levšin*.

with its wings. And so, dear reader, you will hear nothing more from me until the seventh chapter of my book, because I do not speak to anyone in my sleep. I wish you goodnight ... Goodbye. I'm off to sleep." In transitions such as this there is sometimes a confusion between the oral and written convention, which one does not find Scarron. The added complication in *The Mocker* is that Čulkov, the author, is in fact one step removed from the reader, for he has interposed an oral narrator between himself and the reader.

Such digressions reinforce the undercutting narrative irony, which is one of the salient features of the frame story. Ladon playfully announces that he knows how to court a young lady (in this case, Alenona) because he has read novels, which "reform foolish people and turn them into idiots".[24] In courting the fair Alenona he delivers an impassioned declaration of love upon his knees, but feels acutely uncomfortable the whole time because he is kneeling on a pebble. Then, when his plea has its effect on Alenona, he confesses in an aside that he had composed it from passages in novels and tragedies, and that he really considers it all nonsense.

It is in the longest tale narrated by the monk, however, that we find the greatest number of asides and the best examples of the self-conscious narrator at work. Once again, it is the end of chapters or 'evenings' that seems most likely to generate one of these asides. The student Neox appears to have a fatal attraction for wealthy young women in need of affection. His first conquest is Vladimira, the daughter of the high priest at the temple of Černobog. A rendezvous is arranged and Neox finds himself with a woman in a small, well-furnished room. Neox is astonished by her beauty. Here the chapter ends, but the narrator promises the reader he will learn what happened next "if I don't get too bored with telling the story, and the author is pleased to continue with this book; for he is not bored yet, and the more he writes, the greater becomes his desire to continue these tales." [25] Here we have more than one narrative plane. The monk, who is supposed to be telling the tale to Alenona, promises to continue, and then the author-persona talks about himself and his attitude toward the whole collection of tales.

There is another example of this playing with the work and also with

[24] *Russkaja proza XVIII veka*, p. 102. This aside also introduces the subject of the effect of literature upon the reader, about which more will be said a little later in this chapter.
[25] *Peresmešnik*, III, 184.

the characters by the author-persona a little later in this same tale. Vladimira's father is bloodthirsty and avaricious in spite of his benign and pious exterior. She despises her father and behaves willfully and capriciously; she gives money and jewels to her lover Neox, who pockets them with alacrity: Neox always thinks of his purse rather than his heart. Neox spends the money lavishly and the narrator comments wrily that one can see "no moralizing can keep him from wine".[26] To obtain more money Neox agrees to Vladimira's proposal that he shoot her father, using complex philosophical arguments to justify himself. The plan goes awry and the frightened Neox kills Vladimira's guardian or duenna instead of her father. He is beaten and imprisoned by the priests and bewails his lot, speaking eloquently of the uncertain wheel of fortune in an obvious parodical lament. In spite of his dire circumstances, however, Neox resolves not to do away with himself, since, as the narrator explains: "Anyway, he knew that he was very necessary to me for the continuation of my tale, and to the author for the continuation of this book . . .".[27]

Ladon is exaggeratedly modest in the frame story and makes frequent self-deprecatory remarks. He is often coy. He begins to describe the charms of the sleeping and lightly-clad Alenona, but then stops for fear that his female readers will consider him indiscreet: "And moreover I must take care lest women call me immodest, and deny me the favor which I now have the honor to enjoy."[28] Another example of the coy narrator occurs towards the end of "The Tale of the Origin of the Taffeta Beauty Spot". Neox has managed to get himself an influential and lucrative position through acting as a gigolo to the wife of a wealthy merchant. He is saddened at the news that Vladimira has married a local noble, but he makes the acquaintance of another beautiful young lady in circumstances very reminiscent of those surrounding his first meeting with Vladimira. She conceals her identity and insists that they meet in a darkened room. At their first rendezvous the narrator shows the couple meeting, but then tells his reader very regretfully that we must now withdraw and not see what happened next.[29]

It might be pointed out that the use of the coy narrator, fearing that he will be considered indiscreet by his female readers, was by no means

[26] *Ibid.*, 192.
[27] *Peresmešnik*, III, 206.
[28] *Russkaja proza XVIII veka*, p. 109.
[29] *Peresmešnik*, V, 172.

unknown in the Russian manuscript tales. We find what seems to be an echo of the phrase that has just been quoted in the Petrine tale "The Tale of the Russian Nobleman Alexander": "I would say something about them [women], but I am afraid that if I talk scandal, I will remain poor and not have any success with them in the future." [30]

Closely related to the technique of the coy narrator is that of the partially informed narrator, who professes to be giving what he believes to be the facts but admits that he is not absolutely sure if this is actually what happened. Vladimira eventually decides to reveal her identity and so she removes her mask in front of Neox (it had not prevented Neox being overwhelmed by her beauty). The narrator says he does not know precisely when she did this: "After all, one cannot be everywhere at the same time" (*ne vsë v svete usmotret' možno*).[31]

Sometimes the narrator (or author-persona) admits that he knows the facts, but has simply decided not to pass them along to the reader: "I decided it would not be wise to put down here what they said at this time: it alone would have filled a book of enormous size, which I am sure no one would read because it was so huge." [32] On other occasions he will wonder (out loud, as it were) how he should continue his story. At one point in "The Tale of the Origin of the Taffeta Beauty Spot" Neox has departed from Vladimira and traveled to the city of Vineta, where she is due to join him. After Vladimira has set out for the city, the monk is not sure how he should go on with his tale. It is true that ladies should come first, he remarks, but the unfortunate Vladimira is traveling along a very bumpy road and so perhaps it would be best to leave her in peace and instead continue with Neox's adventures a little further along the road to Vineta in the peasant hut where he falls down from the sleeping berth.[33]

Čulkov is certainly displaying here a rather more sophisticated narrative technique that had been known in Russia before his time. If we compare his prose, or rather certain parts of it, with the manuscript tales of the seventeenth and early eighteenth centuries, we are bound to be impressed by Čulkov's superior sense of the narrative possibilities inherent in the prose genres. He explores these possibilities, for example those of rumor and the partially informed narrator, to great effect.

But, passing far beyond the tales as he does, Čulkov fails to solve a

[30] Quoted in G. N. Moiseeva, *Russkie povesti pervoj treti XVIII veka* (Moscow-Leningrad, 1965), p. 187.
[31] *Peresmešnik*, III, 189.
[32] *Ibid.*, 187.
[33] *Ibid.*, IV, 190. See above pp. 95-96.

major problem in *The Mocker*, that of maintaining the fictional world established in the frame story. The Ladon of the frame story, which is narrated in a lively and ironical manner, is quite different from the Ladon who narrates the endless story of Siloslav, with its countless interpolated tales. The young monk, it is true, is recognizably the same type of narrator in the main body of the work as he is when he tells us about his adventures in the frame story. However, as we have seen, his narrative occupies less than a third of *The Mocker* as a whole.

The rhetorical manner of narrating does in large part dispel the illusion of reality, or of a 'real' fictional world, for the narrator or author-persona continually 'lays bare the device' and draws his readers' attention to the fact that he is inventing, simply telling a story. This, however, transfers the main focus of interest from the fictional plot and characters to the only 'real' person, the narrator. But he must then exist as a person for the reader, he must be characterized by his manner of narration, by his asides. At this point we are only a short distance away from a different type of illusion, that of the narrator as a person who really exists. This in its turn leads in later fiction to the narrator as witness, or partial witness, or even as a participant of the events described. More will be said about this use of the narrator in the next chapter, in connection with Čulkov's novel *The Comely Cook*, which is told in the first person.

What, then, is the point of these asides and digressions that occur so frequently in the frame story and the tales narrated by the monk? Is there any purpose or theme that links them together? Such a link is essential if the asides are not soon to become merely facetious and irrelevant; one can get weary very quickly of the 'dear reader' business. An important link in Sterne's novel is Tristram's unavailing struggle against time, his bumbling and complicated attempts to tell what is actually a relatively straightforward story.[34] While Čulkov's efforts are often clumsy and remind us of Sterne's minor predecessors rather than of Sterne himself (it is perhaps unfair to take digressions out of context and form a judgment on their efficacy), they are not entirely unsuccessful or indiscriminate. The link in *The Mocker* is provided by Čulkov's attitude towards prose fiction and towards the purpose of literature as a whole. The link may be a rather tenuous one at times, but it is present.

Čulkov was certainly interested in and amused by the possibilities of prose fiction. The monk comments occasionally on the omnipotence of

[34] Wayne C. Booth, *The Rhetoric of Fiction*, pp. 229-240.

the author of fiction. At one point he notes that such an author can manipulate his characters and events just as he wishes; he can give a hero a crown and a sweetheart, then take them away again if he feels like it: "And if the hero goes mad as is the custom in novels, then the author can turn the earth upside down and change him into a mythological god; for with a novelist (*romanist*) everything is possible."[35] A little later when the student Neox arrives for an assignation with his mysterious lady admirer, the narrator proceeds to describe the building and its furnishings. He will do this, he says, "because a writer of novels (*sočinitel' romanov*) has to be an historian and not bypass anything that has to do with lying and fairy tales (*vran'ë i basni*)".[36] Again Čulkov hints at the inventiveness of the writer and the use he must make of his imagination.

It will be recalled that Neox spends the money he receives from an aunt on a gargantuan feast and party with some fellow students and young ladies of the town. The young monk describes the early part of the evening's entertainment, but then announces that he will not pursue Neox's escapades with his friends because he knows that some people do not like to read about those of low estate: "And so, in order to avoid bringing boredom to the ears of important people with such a low story (*nizkoe povestvovanie*), I will leave out the other adventures; for I know well enough that our young citizens would rather read romances (*romany*) than tales (*skazki*)."[37] This is an interesting comment, but puzzling too, since the monk's own story is called a *skazka.* It suggests that tales were regarded as a 'low' genre by an important group of Russian readers at that period, presumably young members of the nobility in the two capitals. By 'romances', at least in this instance, Čulkov seems to mean the French heroic novels of adventure, or perhaps novels of high society (the terminology is not easy to keep distinct in English either). This was essentially the view of Lomonosov and also of Sumarokov. Although Čulkov was not writing a novel or romance, he was aware of the public's taste for a certain type of fiction and he set out to cater to it, in spite of the disfavor in which novels

[35] *Peresmešnik*, III, 170. We mentioned earlier (Chapter II, p. 40) that the Russian word *roman* was used for both "novel" and "romance". Sometimes Čulkov seems to want to draw a distinction between them, but at others he does not.

[36] *Peresmešnik*, III, 174.

[37] *Peresmešnik*, III, 167. Readers of Gogol' will probably find that many of the asides in the monk's tales sound familiar. This is a case in point. Towards the beginning of Chapter II of *Dead Souls* one can find a very similar statement after the description of Čičikov's two servants, Selifan and Petruška.

(romances) were held by the leading literary figures of the time, and, let it be added, in spite of what was to all appearances his own preference for the ironical, burlesque mode.

Čulkov displayed his interest in prose fiction by writing it. He did not share the moral reservations expressed by the Russian neo-classicists such as Sumarokov. However, there is one digression in "The Tale of the Origin of the Taffeta Beauty Spot" which reads like an extended rider to Sumarokov's condemnation of novels/romances, mentioned at the beginning of Chapter II. After introducing Vladimira as the spoiled and willful daughter of the high priest in Novgorod (apparently not only the city but also the university at which Neox is studying existed in pre-Christian times), the narrator adds in a serious manner:

The fact that Vladimir acted with such ardor in matters of love resulted from her being a young society lady who knew a great more than was good for her; she read romances (novels?) and from them learned to despise people and put on airs before everyone. She learned to consider important things as rubbish, and to behave in a way that shame and delicacy forbid; she learned how to make her young lady friends laugh, but only those who were cleverer than she; she realized how to despise her faith and native land, and to love foreign deceivers; in a word everything that is part of a depraved woman of fashion.[38]

This quotation is rather out of character, for I think we are on fairly safe ground in arguing that Čulkov felt that literature by its moralizing cannot correct or improve human conduct. But perhaps if literature cannot improve, it can corrupt?

Somewhat later in this tale when the student Neox becomes the gigolo of a merchant's wife, the monk stresses that the woman had not been corrupted by novels or any other genre of literature:

Many people say that young girls learn how to attract shallow young men (*ver'xogljady*), that is, lovers, by reading romances (*romany*) and love stories (*basni*); but this worthy citizen's wife without understanding or reading a single worldly book fell in love so heartily that she could occupy the foremost place in Ovid's *Metamorphoses*. . . .[39]

There is little doubt that Čulkov did not believe literature had any moral value, and this view is of course diametrically opposed to a corner-stone of neo-classical aesthetics, as Čulkov himself could not help but be aware. He states his own opinion in clear terms at the outset of his career in the Foreword to *The Mocker*:

[38] *Peresmešnik*, III, 186.
[39] *Peresmešnik*, IV, 218.

In this book there is very little pomposity or moralizing indeed. The book, as I see it, is not capable of improving vulgar manners; on the other hand, there is nothing in it that will make them worse. And so, setting both those matters aside, it will serve to pass the time when people are bored, if they take the trouble to read it.[40]

Later, towards the end of the frame story, when he is satirizing the brutish Balaban, the colonel's nephew, and his hopelessly clumsy and ridiculous attempts to pay court to some unfortunate and unsuspecting young lady, the narrator Ladon mentions that Balaban had some books in his possession which he tried to read, but with a marked lack of success. Balaban decides to sell some of the rather more serious books in order to buy elegant gifts for his beloved. The first volume he decides to exchange is Fénelon's *Les aventures de Télémaque*; he is delighted to get a black taffeta mantilla for it. In a footnote the narrator notes:

One should not be surprised that Balaban was able to buy a mantilla with the money he obtained for Télémaque, because such books are very expensive in our country. . . . We have very few such very old books, and especially books of the Télémaque type; but I will not make any comment here as to why that should be so.[41]

The latter phrase has a sting to it. Obviously enough Čulkov is poking fun at this type of weighty and moralizing novel. It should be recalled that in their attacks on the novel genre both Lomonosov and Sumarokov excluded this work from their general strictures.

We find frequent ironical comments on moralizing and the 'message' the reader is supposed to take away with him from the text. These occur throughout the tales narrated by the young monk, but once more they seem to be more consciously introduced in the longest one "The Tale of the Origin of the Taffeta Beauty Spot" (this tale began to appear in Part III of *The Mocker* which was published in 1768). Two brief examples should serve to illustrate the point. After his financially successful visit with Vladimira, Neox returns to the university again and begins to spend his wealth on another wild party. The narrator turns sadly to his reader and sighs over the young man's behavior: "You can tell that no moral can keep him away from wine."[42] Shortly afterwards, we learn about the plot to kill Vladimira's father. Her duenna, Navera, is blamed for setting Vladimira a bad example; she is a wily old woman who has such a pious exterior and manner that she

[40] *Russkaja proza XVIII veka*, p. 89.
[41] *Russkaja proza XVIII veka*, p. 123.
[42] *Peresmešnik*, III, 192.

has managed to fool even the high priest himself, a master dissembler in his own right. Promised more money, Neox agrees to kill the high priest while he is out on a late night walk in the garden. Neox tries to fortify himself with wine, and is so drunk and terrified when the time comes that he shoots Navera, who is accompanying the priest on his walk that night. The narrator supplies the mock moral: "This means: Don't dig a ditch for someone else, you'll fall into it yourself first."[43] The tone may be ironical, but of course the narrator IS in fact pointing a moral, only in the form of a pithy, proverbial phrase. Čulkov was very fond of proverbs and apparently found their type of 'moralizing' acceptable. The greatest concentration of proverbs occurs in his journal *This and That* (1769).

The longest and most important statement of Čulkov's views on this matter of the moralizing effect of literature, with particular reference to prose fiction, occurs in this same long tale narrated by the monk. It also is an example of the self-conscious narrator at work and offers a critique of some faults Čulkov saw in the romances of the period. It will be recalled that after the unsuccessful attempt to do away with Vladimira's father, Neox is imprisoned by the priests. He bewails his lot and delivers what is obviously a parodical peroration on Dame Fortune and on the human condition. Having recorded this at great length with tongue in cheek, the narrator explains:

This moralizing (*nravoučenie*) is out of place here, but it constitutes the beauty of the book; rhymes beautify verses, and romances or tales (*romany ili skazki*) are adorned with inappropriate moralizing, preferably taken from some good work.

According to the rules of romances and tales, at this point we should describe the parting of the lovers, how they cursed their lives, wanted to die at once, sought something with which to stab themselves, but in desperation found nothing; wanted to end their lives with poison, but poison takes a long time and so they think again, finally lose consciousness, and instead of fainting fall asleep until they have lost their desire for death, and think of continuing to live, although without their beloved. But I would do better to follow the dictates of common sense and relate what is more sensible and natural (*čto bol'še s razumom i s prirodoju sxodno*).[44]

The 'moralizing' that is attacked here is almost assuredly linked with the unnatural behavior of the heroes and heroines of Fëdor Èmin's novels, which suffered notoriously from this fault. At the same time, Èmin did include many 'messages' in his novels and Čulkov is also

[43] *Peresmešnik*, III, 197. "Ne kopaj dlja druga jamy, sam popadëš' v neë prežde."
[44] *Peresmešnik*, III, 205.

objecting to these. What Čulkov found offensive was the moralizing that weighed down works, which – for example, in prose fiction – halted the narrative flow, and which gave rise to 'pomposity' and to a lack of what is 'sensible and natural'. In other words, we have to deal here with a fairly sensitive and sophisticated critical taste.[45]

From the digression that has been quoted above one can see that romances/novels (*romany*) and tales (*skazki*) are linked together, although earlier Čulkov had appeared to be drawing a distinction between the two, suggesting that the latter were in some way a lower genre and less popular with his more aristocratic readers. This simply illustrates the problem we face in attempting to maintain useful distinctions among prose genres during the eighteenth century. The chief point, however, in this quotation is that Čulkov is positing a new and different type of prose fiction from what had gone before (that is, Èmin's) and, incidentally, from his own tales narrated by Ladon. This would be prose fiction that is 'sensible and natural'. One wonders why Čulkov continued to produce the extraordinary adventures of his ancient 'Slavic' heroes and their equally unnatural ladies. Why did he not always practice what he was preaching, instead of writing prose fiction in the heroic, gallant manner and then parodying it, as in the passage from which we have just quoted? It might be argued that Chaucer and Boccaccio also included stories of very different types, from noble romances to crude anecdotes or anti-romantic *novelle*. But they took care to provide their narrators with different personalities and social origins, which explain their preferences for a certain type of story. Furthermore, both of the earlier writers of collections of tales took considerable pains to digress frequently in order to fill in the background, as it were, and outline the circumstances in which the various tales are being told. In other words, the fictional world created in the frame story, for example, that of a pilgrimage or a group of people thrown together for a period because of an epidemic, is maintained throughout the work. Thus it acts as a structural framework to hold the various tales together. As we have already noted, Čulkov has only two narrators and his frame story is not developed, although it is successful as far as it goes.

It should be remembered that Čulkov was still in his twenties when he wrote and published the first four parts of *The Mocker*: he was undergoing his literary apprenticeship. What I have referred to as the

[45] Towards the end of his life Čulkov changed his mind on some of these points. As we saw in Chapter I, he recommended a number of moralizing works to his son.

idealistic prose tradition certainly had an appeal for Čulkov at this time. In 1769 he published his short novel about the life of Achilles before the Trojan War, which is also written in this same manner. However, in spite of its appeal and the obvious influence that its great popularity among his readers would have exercised upon him, his own work in this style is largely derivative. Čulkov seems to have realized this. Certainly the telling parodies that he directed against his own work were bound to have their effect upon him and his views on prose fiction. It is quite interesting to note that, although it is true that Ladon narrates seventy of the one hundred 'evenings' in *The Mocker*, his percentage of the narrative declines as the work proceeds. So, for example, Ladon narrates fully forty of the first forty-five evenings, but only thirty of the remaining fifty-five evenings. This means that the monk, with his burlesque and ironical manner of narrating, at least holds him own in the second part of the work; and of course, we must realize that whatever his feelings, Čulkov could not have abandoned Ladon's narrative completely without destroying whatever semblance of structural coherence the work possessed. What does seem clear is that Čulkov gradually began to demonstrate his preference for the burlesque or ironical manner of narration in the third and fourth parts of the work, which were published in 1768. Although the two types of narrative are kept separate in *The Mocker*, there is a hint of a break in the dichotomy as early as the frame story, that is, in 1766. This takes place in the short interpolated tale entitled "Sharing Someone Else's Headache ("V čužom piru poxmel'e")." [46] Significantly, the break does not occur in the strictly idealistic romance of Ladon in the main body of the work, although the tale is told by Ladon to the colonel's daughter Alenona. What we find in the tale is a blending of the idealistic subject matter that occurs in Ladon's narrative and the ironical tone which is such an important feature of the monk's tales. Two friends, Popal and Milozor ('Goodlooking'), are well-to-do nobles. Milozor loves Popal's wife Prekrasa ('Belle'), but his sense of honor would never permit him to abuse his position, or even to admit his feelings. Up to this point the tale sounds as though it should belong to the idealistic tradition. However, very soon we note that the narrator is not taking the characters at face value, and furthermore we find burlesque references to pagan Slavic mythological figures. For example, Lada, whom Čulkov claims incorrectly as the Slavic pagan goddess of love, is said to be on friendly terms with a serf girl in Popal's house and she helps the girl to shoot arrows into

[46] *Russkaja proza XVIII veka*, 107.

the heart of Milozor. Milozor tries to gain the girl's favors with money and promises to obtain her freedom (note the references to the real situation in Russia at that time; the tale is supposed to be set 'in our empire'). When these inducements prove of no avail, Milozor calls upon the assistance of his good friend, to whom the unwilling serf girl belongs. Popal promises to do him this small favor, and the narrator comments: ". . . and that it was sinful they both knew, and I think the author knows it too, but he does not know how the reader will take it. If he is generous, then he will of course forgive the two young friends their weakness." [47] Nowhere in Ladon's narrative about nobles such as Popal and Milozor do we find the narrator addressing his 'dear reader' in this manner.

Popal pretends that he has taken a fancy to the serf girl himself and orders her to appear at a darkened arbor in the garden of his house towards midnight to accede to his desires. On this occasion the girl, with or without the good offices of Lada, is powerless to refuse. Here once again we note some unfamiliar features: the mingling of nobility with servants, and also the suggestion of contemporary Russian reality in the relationship between the lord Popal and his serf girl. It is true that the *droit du seigneur* had been practiced in many countries, but this tale is supposed to be set in mid-eighteenth-century Russia. The distraught serf girl goes to her mistress Prekrasa, who resolves to teach her tyrannical and wayward husband a lesson. She turns up herself for the rendezvous in the darkened arbor, where she is awaited by the amorous Milozor. The comedy of errors is then played out with neither partner knowing who the other really is. When they emerge from the arbor, they discover what has happened, and then confess very nobly to the unfortunate Popal. However, each has a reason to feel guilty and so each apologizes, and the two men remain friends. The tale reminds us of some of the tales in the *Decameron* and may appear rather ordinary, but it is most unusual to find in Čulkov's prose such a combination of noble characters, idealized setting, burlesque references, and tongue-in-cheek narrative tone.

One should also note the contrast between the aristocratic characters and elegant milieu of the tale and the rather vulgar events taking place at the colonel's, both before and after Ladon tells the tale to Alenona. The discovery of the identity of the lovers in the dark arbor recalls the farcical happenings that culminate in the discovery by Ladon of the housekeeper and the young monk in the trunk. We might also note that

[47] *Russkaja proza XVIII veka*, pp. 107-108.

Ladon's own extremely refined and delicate courting of Alenona sets the monk's affair with the housekeeper, and also Balaban's clumsy attempts at courtship, into greater relief.

There would seem to be some justification for arguing that this system of incongruous contrasts is a structural principle in the frame story. It is of interest to recall in this connection what has been noted about the *Decameron* and the later collection of tales entitled *Cent nouvelles nouvelles*, namely that they make extensive use of "ironical commentary and burlesque and comic contrasts: for instance, between aristocratic status and vulgar behavior, between pious speech and lascivious deed".[48] We have certainly discovered something very similar in the frame story and elsewhere in the tales narrated by the monk.

Although further hints of Čulkov's developing critical attitude towards the idealistic manner of narration occur in the main body of *The Mocker* (most notably in the third and fourth volumes which appeared in 1768, two years after the first two volumes), the two types of narrative are kept separate, and it is not until 1769 that we find another example of the blending which has been remarked upon in the short tale "Sharing Someone Else's Headache". This occurs in another brief story, without title, which was published in Čulkov's journal *This and That*.[49] It was presumably written at much the same time as Čulkov was preparing for publication his novelette *The Adventures of Achilles Under the Name of Pyrrha Before the Siege of Troy*, which is narrated in the idealistic manner and owes a great deal to the French romance or heroic novel.[50]

In this tale too Čulkov makes no effort to keep the two types of narrative separate. It tells the story of a young man named Neton (i.e., *net on*, 'he does not exist') who has lost his way in the forest and would have perished had the goddess of the woods not taken pity upon him and led him to a castle. The castle is then described, together with its magnificent grounds. Predictably, Neton comes upon a sleeping beauty who is nude. She awakens and tells Neton that because she helped a brazen young shepherd escape, the castle magicians had turned her

[48] Margaret Schlauch, *Antecedents of the English Novel, 1400-1600 (from Chaucer to Deloney)* (Warsaw, 1963), p. 100.

[49] *I to i së*, Weeks 10, 11, 13, 14, and 15. The tale takes up only part of each of these issues.

[50] *Poxoždenie Axillesovo....* This work must have become available in July, for in the last July issue of his journal (Week 31) Čulkov published an announcement informing his readers that the book was being sold for 20 kopeks "at Vege the bookbinders", where the journal too was sold.

arms and legs into marble, but by waking her Neton has broken the spell. She and her sister are reunited and Neton learns that they are both sorceresses, although they apparently have only moderate powers. They entertain Neton to a feast in gratitude for his opportune arrival. At the feast he is attended by a beautiful maidservant and, again predictably, Neton and the girl fall in love at first sight.

Thus far in the tale we could well be reading a part of Ladon's narrative. All the requisite elements are present: the noble youth, the sorceresses, the exquisite landscape, the magnificent buildings, the magical transformations, and the interference of divine beings in the action. And yet a discordant note is struck by the appearance in the foreground of the maidservant (instead of a princess) and the narrative tone becomes quite different as soon as she enters upon the scene. In speaking of Neton's reactions to her appearance, the narrator says: "A certain passionate agitation overcame his heart, or to put it simply, he fell in love with her at first sight . . .".[51] At once we notice the parody of the lofty phrase so commonly used in the literature of that period, when it was felt necessary to employ a high style in discussing such emotions. We are reminded of Čulkov's undercutting technique: his fondness for presenting material in a lofty manner and then calling a spade a spade.

Neton and Silvia have a series of quite extraordinary adventures, similar to those that occur in Ladon's narrative in *The Mocker*. Neton is turned into a horse.[52] But he is entertained by local society and behaves with decorum "showing that he had attended a school where the social graces were taught (*v kotoroj učat politike domašnej*)".[53] The major difference between this story and those narrated by Ladon is the ironical tone and the social satire it contains. For example, at one point he remarks that dancing masters are received more readily into some homes than are "people versed in literature (*ljudi razumejuščie slovesnye nauki*)".[54]

[51] *I to i së*, Week 11.

[52] Čulkov's story is reminiscent of *The Golden Ass*, a Latin work by Lucius Apuleius, in which the hero is turned into an ass by his impetuous lover and then has a series of adventures that are sometimes similar to those of Neton. It is not at all unlikely that Čulkov knew this work before it appeared in Russian translation in 1780-1781.

[53] *I to i së*, Week 14. Note the obsolete use of *politika*. It is related to the French *politesse*, but probably entered Russian by way of an imprint borrowing from Polish.

[54] *Ibid*. The social satire is fairly traditional. Compare the epigram by Sumarokov:

> Tancovščik! Ty bogat! Professor! Ty ubog.
> Konečno, golova v počten'i men'še nog. (1759)

This tale is longer than the previous one in the frame story and provides a more detailed illustration of the breaking up of the narrative categories which was gradually taking place in Čulkov's prose in the late sixties. What is more, it contains certain features that are absent from the earlier tale – the blend is more complex: there is both serious and comic subject matter, and also both serious and comic narrative tone. So that we have a mingling of subject matter and style. However, Čulkov is still unable to treat 'concrete reality' seriously; it remains for him simply a subject for satire and farce, although the presence in the tale of more social satire, albeit of a rather traditional variety, is an interesting indication that Čulkov was beginning to turn his attention increasingly towards topical subject matter. We also find in this tale a wider range of characters, more particularly of the lower and middling sort, such as military officers and merchants. There is one important feature that is absent from the tale, and this is mythological burlesque: a most interesting development considering what we have said about the monotony of this type of burlesque and the possible inhibiting nature of its influence upon Čulkov's fiction.

Very little attention has been given to this brief tale, possibly because it lies buried in several issues of Čulkov's journal *This and That*, itself a very rare item. And yet, short though it is, the tale of Neton is an accurate guide to Čulkov's development as a prose writer. This did not lie in the direction of the idealistic narrative represented by his novelette *The Adventures of Achilles*, although it was published in the same year of 1769. Both the narrative prose traditions upon which Čulkov drew for inspiration had proven of great value to him, and indeed they continued to play an important role in the development of Russian prose fiction in the eighteenth century. The question now arose as to whether Čulkov, having practiced in both types of narrative separately, would be able to create something of his own by employing the best features of both.

Paul Scarron's influence on Čulkov's treatment of his material and on his narrative technique was in some ways a mixed blessing; or rather one should say that the young Russian author lacked the experience and finesse to take full advantage of what was available to him. Čulkov's growth as a writer of modern fiction was hampered by his addiction to the burlesque, which he found in *Le roman comique*, and the attitude toward literary material drawn recognizably from the contemporary world of Russian reality which the burlesque normally entailed. He tended to ridicule everything; he may make his reader laugh but he does not make him think. Furthermore, Čulkov's introduction of the rhetorical manner, although refreshing in the context of Russian fiction of that period, was on occasion too indiscriminate and his narrators were not adequately identified and characterized by their digressions.

At the same time, the positive aspects of Scarron's influence ought not to be forgotten. It might well be that because of his reading of Scarron, as well as some of the manuscript tales, Čulkov did not engage exclusively in the writing of fabulous romances. Parody of certain features of one's own work may indicate lack of orientation and confusion of ideas, but it also serves a useful function as a catalyst in creating new genres, themes and modes, and in helping to discard outworn attitudes. This process is understandably not a smooth one and in Čulkov's case there was considerable backsliding; yet as we have seen in the two short stories just discussed, there was from the outset of his writing career a critical or at least ambivalent attitude toward the romance and the one-sided, idealistic manner of narration. Related to this is the gain in aesthetic distance which accrues from the use of the self-conscious narrator in comic fiction, about which more will be said in the next chapter.

V

THE COMELY COOK

It is of some interest to find in Russian literature, as in Čulkov's own career, a steady development of prose genres similar to that in other literatures, namely the development from anecdote to short story to tale (or *novella*) to novel. This is not merely a matter of length, although that is important enough, but also a matter of structure, complexity, and subject matter. The peculiarity of the Russian development is that it was so compressed; we have seen an excellent example of this compression in the case of Čulkov.

The modern European novel since the eighteenth century has been essentially an extended piece of narrative prose concerned with a group of people in a definite place and at a definite time, and it has been much concerned with man and his relationship to his own society and to his own time and place. It is also a vital part of the novelistic tradition that the author must make his reader believe that what he relates actually happened and that his characters really existed. To create this illusion of reality, or at least to persuade the reader to 'suspend his disbelief', the author employs any of a number of narrative devices. One such device is the first-person discourse, in which a literary persona relates directly to the reader a series of events that happened to him.

From the purely literary standpoint Čulkov's novel *The Comely Cook, or the Adventures of a Depraved Woman* is the most satisfying of his works for the modern reader.[1] Although one can certainly discern some picaresque elements in it and also the influence of Le Sage in some aspects of the plotting, these will not concern me in this chapter.[2]

[1] *Prigožaja povarixa, ili poxoždenie razvratnoj ženščiny*, Part I (St. Petersburg, 1770). An English translation of the novel is now available in Harold B. Segel, ed., *The Literature of Eighteenth-Century Russia*, II (Dutton Paperback; New York, 1967), pp. 28-68.

[2] The picaresque elements in the novel and in some parts of *The Mocker* have been thoroughly investigated by Jurij Striedter in his study: *Der Schelmenroman in Russland* (Berlin, 1961). Striedter often steps outside the picaresque framework of his study to make other valuable comments about the novel.

I do not think we can accept the brash condemnation of the novel made by N. Belozerskaja, who referred to it as "nothing more than a weak imitation of the lightweight French novel (*slaboe podražanie francuzskim romanam lëgkogo soderžanija*)." [3] This comment was made in the latter part of the nineteenth century when it was an axiom of scholarship that Russian literature of the preceding centure was almost totally imitative. Belozerskaja claimed for Vasilij Narežnyj the title of the first Russian novelist, thus following in the footsteps of Belinskij and others. She writes: "It is only in *The Russian Gil Blas*, Narežnyj's first major work in 1814, that we see a definite turn towards the creation of a completely Russian novel.[4] Given the title of Narežnyj's novel, it is perhaps a rather unfortunate choice as a candidate for the honor bestowed upon it. Without wishing to get involved in a futile argument, I would suggest that Čulkov's novel ought not to be dismissed as a mere imitation simply because it contains elements which were and are common in European fiction. There is little doubt that it is a novel and that it is firmly based in Russian reality, something which cannot be said for the somewhat earlier romances of Fëdor Èmin. To place the rise of the indigenous Russian novel in 1814 is to disregard Čulkov's achievement. Although *The Comely Cook* has been, and will probably remain, purely of scholarly interest (it has never been widely known among the general reading public), it has often been praised and with justice. It is no exaggeration to say with a scholar who wrote some fifty years ago that *The Comely Cook* stands out from the prose fiction of this period as 'the unique work of art in the eighteenth century'.[5]

If it is a characteristic of the modern novel that it is set in a definite place (or places) and at a definite time (often the author's own), that it attempts to be credible, then Čulkov's work is most certainly a novel, and indeed the first novel produced by a Russian. The setting of the novel presents a sharp contrast to those 'misty Varangian times' in Ladon's narrative, which are indeed also the setting of the monk's longest tale, "The Tale of the Origin of the Taffeta Beauty Spot". It is quite true that in the frame story and in a few of the short stories narrated by the monk there are references to Russian reality, to cities

[3] N. Belozerskaja, *Vasilij Trofimovič Narežnyj. Istoriko-literaturnyj očerk*, 2nd ed. rev. (St. Petersburg, 1896), p. 38. This is a very useful pioneer study, but rather opinionated: the author is for example inexcusably biased against Nikolaj Karamzin.

[4] Belozerskaja, *op. cit.*, pp. 3-4.

[5] Ekaterina Mečnikova, "Na zare russkogo romana", *Golos Minuvšego*, VI (1914), 25. This article remains one of the best introductions to the subject.

such as Moscow, St. Petersburg, and Astrakhan', but for the most part we are swept along from magical abodes to pagan temples, in a world of 'ancient Slavs', sorceresses, long voyages on the backs of dolphins, transformations, and so on. In neither the frame story nor in any of the tales narrated by the monk do we have such a consistent and deliberate attempt to 'place' the characters and events in the real world of contemporary Russia as is made in this novel. Furthermore, Russian reality is not despised, it is simple there; no need is felt to 'elevate' it by using mock-heroic or high burlesque.[6]

Right at the outset Martona, the comely cook who relates her own adventures, tells us that her husband, a sergeant, had been killed at the Battle of Poltava. Poltava, a small town in the Ukraine, was the site of the battle in June, 1709 in which Peter the Great defeated Charles XII of Sweden. Martona tells us further that she was widowed at nineteen and left in Kiev, also in the Ukraine, with no one to turn to:

> Everyone knows that we won a victory at Poltava, and at that battle my unfortunate husband was killed. He wasn't a noble and did not own any villages and so I was left without any way of earning a living. I bore the title of sergeant's wife, but I was poor. I was nineteen years old at the time, so my poverty seemed even more unbearable to me.[7]

If Martona was nineteen when her husband was killed at Poltava, she must have been born in 1690. The events she is describing therefore do not take place at the time the novel was published, but some sixty years earlier.

After the loss of her husband Martona is disconsolate for two weeks, but then 'an honorable old woman' known throughout Kiev offers to find her a protector. For two days Martona refuses to follow the procuress' advice, but then gives way. Here one notes that exact times are given. Her first lover is a butler who steals from his master. He and Martona employ a young boy and girl as servants, and she enjoys playing the lady, terrorizing the maid. Soon Martona moves up in the

[6] Although Russian reality is described and mentioned in *The Comely Cook*, no attempt is made to describe the characters' immediate surroundings in any detail, that is, their clothing, the rooms where they meet. The novel is not what the French call "un roman bien meublé". This results in part from the fact that it is a first-person narrative.

[7] *Russkaja proza XVIII veka*, ed. A. V. Zapadov and G. P. Makogonenko, Vol. I (Moscow-Leningrad, 1950), 159. I shall use this text of the novel. It is also available in V. L. Barcev, *Obstojatel'noe bibliografičeskoe opisanie...*, V (St. Petersburg, 1901), 187-210 (portrait of Čulkov on p. 188); and in *Prigožaja povarixa*, ed. A. A. Titov (Moscow, 1904). Of the latter edition only 250 copies were printed; the Widener Library at Harvard has a copy.

world and becomes the mistress of Sveton (a name related to *svet* 'society'), who is the butler's master. Sveton is a wealthy noble and treats Martona with elaborate respect. She remarks: "I was quite amazed to find that one night had made me the mistress and sovereign of my former master." [8] When the butler suggests that they work together to steal from Sveton, Martona agrees: ". . . virtue was completely unknown to me." [9] Soon Sveton is required by his father to go to his home in the country and he tells Martona, rather late in the day, that he is married. He had been obliged by his parents to marry a woman he did not love. Sveton proposes that Martona leave Kiev also and stay at the home of a friend's brother, pretending to be a close relative of the friend's wife. Sveton can then visit her since the distance between the two houses is only six versts – again the exact distance is given. Somewhat later, when she has become the housekeeper of a retired colonel in Moscow, Martona takes the trouble to tell us the precise location of the colonel's house. And right at the end of the novel, when Martona goes to visit a former lover who is dying, once again we are told the distance she had to travel: some twenty versts. This mentioning of distances and periods of time, and of places, is something new in Čulkov's fiction. It is done in an offhand manner, which however helps to create the illusion of reality.

Čulkov's novel was the only major work that he published anonymously. Its title page announced that it was Part I, but no further part or parts ever appeared and we do not know whether Čulkov ever got as far as putting down a continuation on paper. One quite often comes across the statement in literary histories that Čulkov wrote a second part, which was forbidden publication by Catherine's censorship. There seems to be little or no evidence to support this statement, but scholars still seem reluctant to omit the possibility that a second part of the novel was censored. The editors of a collection of eighteenth-century prose published in 1950 declare: "A second part was either not written or did not appear because it was censored." [10] Čulkov promised a sixth part of *The Mocker*, but did not produce it; all we can say in the case of both it and *The Comely Cook* is that no continuations exist, although we have every reason to believe Čulkov intended to provide them. We cannot know why he returned to *The Mocker* to produce a fifth part after twenty years, but never returned to his novel. The lack of a con-

[8] *Russkaja proza XVIII veka*, p. 163.
[9] *Loc. cit.*
[10] *Russkaja proza XVIII veka*, p. 84.

tinuation is more acutely felt in the case of *The Comely Cook*, because certain narrative tensions are created and then not fully explored. At the end of Part I, one of Martona's former lovers, believing mistakenly that he had killed her protector in a duel, takes poison and lies dying, with Martona in attendance. The reader is bound to wonder what effect the death of the man will have upon her relationship with her protector and indeed upon her own personality, since she seems so affected by the man's suicide.

In the case of this novel, as with his collection of "Slavic Tales", we have to deal with a series of complex influences, both domestic and foreign. The use of a first-person narrator is a case in point. First-person narratives are not uncommon in the native Russian manuscript tales and an attempt has been made recently by a Czech scholar to link Čulkov's novel to this tradition.[11] However, the autobiographical genre was far more widely known in Western European fiction, particularly among the picaresque novelists; Čulkov may well have been prompted to write an *Ich-Erzählung* by the example of such writers as Le Sage, whose novel *Gil Blas* first appeared in Russian translation in 1754-1755. But it should be noted that Čulkov had already long shown a preference for first-person narrators. The frame story in *The Mocker* is narrated by Ladon, and one could say that the whole of this work is narrated by a first-person narrator, or narrators: Ladon and the monk. However, the best examples of first-person discourse occur in the frame story and in Ladon's narrative, which includes a number of interpolated tales wherein a character tells his or her own story. A first-person narrator is also used by Čulkov in some parts of his three burlesque poems that were published in his journal *This and That*. Consequently, in this instance we may be dealing with an example of 'self-influence'. An important point to note, however, is that in his novel Čulkov displayed far greater skill in first-person discourse than he had ever done before in his earlier fiction (or in his verse). This is a point I will come back to a little later in this chapter.

The extended monologue is very common in the romances of Èmin and is really the only form of characterization that is consistently used; it is one of the main features of Èmin's prose fiction. Martona is naturally quite different from the models of feminine virtue who tell their

[11] Světla Mathauserová, *Ruský zdroj monologické románové formy (M. D. Čulkov)* (Prague, 1961). There is a Russian summary. Mathauserová mentions in particular a manuscript work "Roman v stixax" ("Novel in Verse") and the *azbukovniki*. I am indebted to Professor D. Tschiżewskij of the University of Heidelberg for bringing this monograph to my attention.

stories in Èmin's romances; one could say that Čulkov's novel is a parody, for he goes out of his way to have Martona confess openly to her sins and her weakness when faced with temptations: one cannot imagine Martona hesitating to choose a fate worse than death rather than death itself. Although in Čulkov's novel the parodical elements do not intrude and are not essential to an understanding of it or an appreciation of its merits, they may explain why it was referred to as a 'satirical novel' (*satiričeskij roman*) in a list of his works printed at the end of Part IV of his *Collection of Various Songs* in 1774.[12]

Čulkov's selection of a woman narrator was remarkably precocious for a Russian at that time, although once again we should not neglect the native sources that Čulkov might have drawn upon in deciding to use an immoral heroine as his narrator. It is not at all unlikely that he was at least partially influenced by the brief satirical poems, frequently written as female monologues, that were quite popular at that period. His friend and literary collaborator Mixail Popov wrote several of these short poems, known as 'epigrams', and it is most interesting from our point of view that Čulkov published some of them in his journal *This and That* (1769). For example, Čulkov published three such poems by Popov in Week 7 and the last of these was written as a female monologue:

Пожалуй перестань любовь мне толковать;
Я знаю, как любить, и верной быть кому:
Богатым сердце я привыкла отдавать,
А не тому,
Таскает кто суму.
Без денег верной быть скажу я без приветов,
Пустая выдумка одних у нас поэтов.[13]

However, one must say that this provides us with only the broadest sort of hint of what Čulkov was able to do with his female narrator. Martona is quite a complex personality, and her attitude towards life and love cannot be summed up in a few lines. There was a tradition of the wicked and deceitful woman going back a long way in Russian literature, but no comparable tradition in which women were portrayed

[12] *Sobranie raznyx pesen*, Part IV (St. Petersburg, 1774), facing p. 236. This list is the most complete before that in the second edition of Čulkov's *Ekonomičeskie zapiski* in 1790. It may also have been composed by Čulkov himself and submitted to the publishers.

[13] "I beg you, stop telling me about love; I know how to love and to whom I must be true; My custom is to give my heart to rich men, And not one Who carries around a beggar's bag. I say straight to your face that being faithful without money Is just a mere fiction invented by our poets."

sympathetically, although women are treated favorably in some later manuscript tales, for example, "The Tale of Jul'jana Osor'ina", "Karp Sutulov", and the romances of the Petrine and post-Petrine period. Of course Russia had experienced nothing similar to the age of chivalry with its cult of courtly love and the idealized female, nor a period of literature comparable to that of seventeenth-century France. As has been noted by F. C. Green: "The moral ascendancy of the Frenchwoman in literature was never so complete as during the period beginning with the Fronde and ending with the seventeenth century." [14] In French literature we note a growing interest in the female personality from the time of Madame de Lafayette, and the same is true of English literature.

One of the interesting aspects of *The Comely Cook* is that with it Čulkov began to become more obviously a part of his century as a writer of prose. As we saw with his earlier work, he had previously tended to belong to the seventeenth century. Now, with his novel, which demonstrates his interest in the female personality and in first-person discourse, Čulkov takes his place among other prose writers of the period, particularly those in France and England. This closing of the cultural gap of which I spoke in an earlier chapter was reflected in other genres and among other authors in Russia at this time.

Comparisons and contrasts between Čulkov's novel and other first-person narratives produced in Western Europe suggest themselves at once. It is fascinating to find that the best French novels of the eighteenth century were almost all first-person narratives; one thinks of *Gil Blas, Manon Lescaut, La Nouvelle Héloïse, Les Liaisons dangeureuses,* and particularly of *La vie de Marianne* by Marivaux, because unlike the earlier novels in our list this novel is narrated by a woman. Marivaux's novel, or rather the first three parts of it, was translated into Russian and published in 1762.[15] It is tempting to believe that Čulkov read this work and then set about producing his 'life of Martona'. Of course Marianne is no harlot like Martona, but she does get into some rather compromising situations. It is not the morals of the two women which are of interest here, but the technical matter of first-person discourse by a woman. From Marivaux Čulkov may have obtained the idea of a woman writing down her story several years after the events she describes had taken place. However, Čulkov does not take the

[14] F. C. Green, *French Novelists, Manners and Ideas* (New York, 1929), p. 16.
[15] *Žizn' Marianny, ili Poxoždenija gospoži grafini de ****, Vol. I (Moscow, 1762).

trouble to frame his novel very elaborately, and so the reader is likely to be puzzled by the fact that Martona, the wife of a sergeant, is such an accomplished writer, and may also wonder why she is writing down her adventures and how they came to be published. If Čulkov did read *La vie de Marianne*, he does not seem to have noticed the care Marivaux took to frame his story and clear up these matters in order to further the illusion that Marianne was a real person. It will be recalled that Marivaux says that he found the manuscript of Marianne's adventures and had been persuaded to publish it by some friends:

> Il y a six mois que j'achetai une maison de campagne à quelques lieus de Rennes, qui, depuis trente ans, a passé successivement entre les mains de cinq ou six personnes. J'ai voulu faire changer quelque chose à la disposition du premier appartement, et dans une armoire pratiquée dans l'enforcement d'un mur, on y a trouvé un manuscrit en plusieurs cahiers contenant l'histoire qu'on va lire, et le tout d'une écriture de femme.

One notes here that Marivaux subtly says that it was not actually he who found the manuscript. He also goes on to say that no one knows who Marianne was: he is wise not to go into too many details.

It is perhaps less likely that Čulkov had read *Moll Flanders* by Daniel Defoe. This novel was not available in Russian before 1770, but it is possible that Čulkov was familiar with a French version, which appeared in 1761.[16] Again, there is no concrete evidence that Čulkov had read Defoe's novel, but one is tempted by the similarities at least to consider the possibility that he may have borrowed the idea of a woman narrator of easy virtue from Defoe. Like Marivaux, Defoe has taken the trouble to frame his novel and his heroine, like Marianne, is writing down her adventures several years after the events being described.

The moralizing of Defoe's novel would certainly have repelled Čulkov, for we have seen that it is characteristic of him to decline to moralize or even to believe that literature has a moral value. The main distinction between Moll and Martona is that the Russian woman is completely realistic about her behavior; she makes no pretense to be what she is not. An important link between both novels is that, although in their form they owe something to the picaresque tradition, their heroines are clearly shown to be products of their respective environments and are characterized with greater subtlety than the normal *picaro*. As Ian Watt has said, the typical picaresque hero is "not so

[16] *Mémoires et aventures de Mlle Moll Flanders* (London, Nourse, 1761). Quoted in H. W. Streeter, *The Eighteenth Century English Novel in French Translation: A Bibliographical Study* (New York, 1936), p. 61.

much a complete personality whose actual life experiences are significant in themselves as a literary convention for the presentation of a variety of satiric observations and comic episodes."[17] The picaresque tradition has been long-lived and the picaresque framework occurs in many novels, but there comes a point when one has to decide whether in a given novel this provides a fruitful context in which to discuss its special features. For example, can one really do justice to Gogol' 's *Dead Souls* by approaching it as a picaresque novel, even though it is certainly structured like one?

The first-person narrative can provide the writer with an excellent opportunity for creating an individual instead of a mere type or mouthpiece for a given vice or virtue. And it is particularly useful if the narrator is not morally perfect. To quote Wayne C. Booth: "We have seen that inside views can build sympathy for the most vicious character. When properly used, this effect can be of immeasurable value in forcing us to see the human worth of a character whose actions, objectively considered, we would deplore ...".[18]

It is because we have an 'inside view' of Martona that we know a great deal more about her than we do of any of Čulkov's other characters, whether they are rogues or not. One can see this more clearly if one compares the way certain characters and episodes are treated in *The Mocker* and in *The Comely Cook*. During the frame story the young renegade monk tells us his life story. One of his escapades entails an amorous adventure with a young woman who has just become a widow. In this case the story is told from the point of view of the monk, or the triumphant male, and it is told with the appropriate touch of farcical detail and callousness. However, in *The Comely Cook* another young widow is allowed to tell the story from HER point of view. She becomes for us not a figure of fun or the subject of ribald jokes, but a human being with a lot of faults and some virtues; in other words, what E. M. Forster called a 'round' character, as opposed to the 'flat' characters of Čulkov's earlier works in prose. Equally important, in the context of Čulkov's development, is that Martona is of modest social origin and very much a part of the Russian scene at that time, and yet she is not treated satirically, but with a measure of seriousness.

[17] Ian Watt, *The Rise of the Novel* (Los Angeles and Berkeley, 1962), p. 94. Watt is arguing that *Moll Flanders* is not a picaresque novel, but belongs rather to a post-picaresque tradition.

[18] Wayne C. Booth, *The Rhetoric of Fiction* (Chicago, 1961), p. 378.

We have several indications that Martona is writing her story several years after the events she describes. It is a vital fact, seemingly ignored by all previous commentators on the novel, that Martona, the heroine of the story, is not altogether the same person as Martona, the narrator. She is not writing down her adventures as they happen, nor is she keeping a diary. She has evidently become familiar with society and acquired some culture, and it should be remembered that she may well have become quite wealthy, because at the end of the novel (or of the first part of it) the dying Axal', one of her former lovers, returns some money and jewels to her and gives her the deeds to an estate. There are therefore hints as to the possible reasons for the skill Martona displays in telling her story.

Martona is looking back, telling us what happened to her in the past when she was a young woman. At one point in the novel Martona finds herself in Moscow and feels sad because she is alone and has lost her former lover, Sveton. She tells us that she 'foolishly' burst into tears, and compares her naivety as a young women with the knowing ways of the present younger generation: "Nowadays girls of my type (*naši sëstry*) don't behave like that. They always want to get rid of one noble gentleman as quickly as possible, so as to search out another one right away and begin living a life of luxury . . .".[19] Here Martona is suggesting that in her youth she was not so self-seeking and hard-hearted as the young women of today, that is, the time at which she is writing. She goes on to say that one could not find a single girl of her sort in the whole country without three or four lovers at one and the same time.

Martona not only compares herself favorably as a young woman with the young women of her type at the time she is writing. She also seems to consider that she has become as it were a 'different person' from what she had been when she was having the adventures she describes. We can see this by the way she uses the past tense at certain points in the course of the novel. For example, at the beginning of her story when her first lover, the butler, suggests that they work together in order to rob from Sveton, the butler's master who has taken his place as her protector, Martona agrees: ". . . virtue was completely unknown to me."[20] The point here is that Martona the narrator considers herself not so immoral as he used to be, that is, not so immoral as Martona the heroine of the book. If she were writing down her adventures soon

[19] *Russkaja proza XVIII veka*, p. 167.
[20] *Ibid.*, p. 163.

after the event, or in the form of a diary, then she would not be able to adopt the attitude to her behavior that she does. An immoral (even more so an amoral) young woman such as Martona the heroine would not keep repeating, as Martona the narrator does, that she WAS immoral, that she DID not know the meaning of virtue and gratitude. We understand that Martona the narrator is capable of looking at her former behavior objectively when she says for example: "I did not know the meaning of gratitude; I had not heard about it from anyone, and thought that one could live on earth without it", or again: "I was one of those beautiful women who believe they are obliged to no one and dispense their favors with magnanimity." [21]

Perhaps because she now considers herself a different person, now and then Martona will seek to justify her actions as a young woman. Although she is very frank about her behavior, on occasion she seems to feel the need to make it clear that she was not as bad as all that. At one point she draws a most literary comparison between the inconstancy of the elements and the world of nature on the one hand and the inconstancy of women on the other, and then pleads: "How can a woman, who is born to change, love one man until she dies." [22] It is perfectly true that Martona is by no means a predatory female, preying upon every man she meets. Sveton waits until they are on their way into the country before telling her that he is married, and when they are discovered in *flagrante delicto* near his estate in the country by his enraged wife, Sveton simply runs away and leaves Martona to take a drubbing and get thrown out onto the street without a penny to her name. Later in the novel another man named Axal' persuades her to steal from her aged protector, a retired colonel, pretending that they can then elope and get married, but he takes everything for himself and abandons her.[23] Martona remarks in her own defense: "I think that even sinful women are not entirely without sense (*rassudok*), and if they were not overcome by inconstancy and their desire for luxury, then of course they might be more virtuous than usurers and misers." [24]

Martona comes across some quite unsavory characters and she is acute enough to see how hypocritical they are (perhaps not at the time?). For example, after being thrown out by the wife of Sveton, Martona sets out for Moscow, where she becomes a cook in the house of a cer-

[21] *Russkaja proza XVIII veka*, pp. 164 and 171.
[22] *Ibid.*, p. 171.
[23] Čulkov still uses invented names for his characters in the traditional neoclassical manner.
[24] *Russkaja proza XVIII veka*, p. 177.

tain Secretary, an unusually pious man: "Every morning he knelt at prayer for two hours, while his wife was in the front room practicing bribery and accepting all sorts of gifts." [25] The Secretary's wife is highly promiscuous and is drunk all day every day except for a short period when she wakes up in the morning. Her husband does not mind at all about her promiscuity; he only wants to be sure that she helps him accept bribes, so that he does not have to soil his hands. Martona, as she herself points out, does not suffer from the sin of drinking. Martona may well be a 'depraved woman' but Čulkov seems determined to show us that there are degrees of depravity. It is quite obvious that the promiscuous and alcoholic Secretary's wife is introduced to act as a character foil. The same is true of the second woman with whom Martona comes into close contact. This is the noblewoman who is married to a wealthy merchant. Martona is implicitly contrasted and compared to this woman, and she can hardly fail to come off best in the comparison, for the merchant's wife tries to poison him.

A character like Martona is something completely new in Čulkov's fiction. She has both good and bad qualities, and this relative complexity of personality differentiates her not only from other female characters in *The Comely Cook*, but also from all Čulkov's earlier heroines, both those in Ladon's narrative and those in the monk's tales. Martona is no model of feminine virtue like Prelepa or Askliada, but neither is she like a young woman such as Vladimira, who plots the murder of her own father. In fact Martona is instrumental in preventing the murder of the merchant by his noble wife. When she learns of the wife's plot, she at once informs her lover Svidal' so that they can put a stop to it. Svidal' behaves with tact and firmness in helping to reveal to the merchant his wife's plot. Martona tells us that Svidal' did this purely out of sympathy for the unfortunate merchant, not in any hope of personal gain. The merchant's wife entertains many so-called poets constantly (they are her lovers), and permits things to take place in his house to which even Martona takes exception. Among the noblewoman's guests are an old man seeking to seduce a young girl of thirteen, and a young man trying to marry a wealthy old woman with one foot in the grave. Martona says she considers the noblewoman's salon 'a school of love, or a house of sin'.[26]

Martona's manner of narration recalls that in the monk's tales rather

[25] *Russkaja proza XVIII veka*, p. 165.
[26] *Ibid.*, p. 184.

than that in Ladon's narrative (the frame story is, however, also narrated by Ladon). She does occasionally turn to her 'dear reader' as the narrator is in the habit of doing in some parts of *The Mocker*. A typical example occurs in the early part of the novel when the butler proposes to Martona that they both work together to steal from Sveton. She says that she agreed to the plan, but something prevented them from putting it into practice: "And what that obstacle was the reader will soon learn, if he is not yet bored by reading my adventures."[27] There is also a hint of Čulkov's earlier technique of playing the partially informed narrator, when Martona says that she is not sure whether Axal' went into town to buy a woman's dress as a disguise or sent his servant to pick it up for him.[28] However, Martona does not normally employ such techniques. She does not draw attention to the mechanics of narration as the monk does in his "Tale of the Origin of the Taffeta Beauty Spot". In the monk's tale the toying with the plot or 'laying bare the device', as the Russian Formalists called it, was of great interest but one sensed that it was finally leading into a blind alley, since the reader never really got close to the narrator as a 'real' person, as was pointed out in the previous chapter. It is significant that in *The Comely Cook* the auctorial intrusions are completely absent; Martona is left alone with her reader. Ideally, then, her narrative manner and her digressions should belong to her and characterize her.

Since Martona is looking back over a period of years to her life as a young woman, she is able to relate her adventures with a certain detachment. Thus, although Čulkov himself does not comment on characters and events, he can introduce a 'moral voice' and an angle of vision on them. She employs an ironical and sometimes bantering tone which is reminiscent of that used in the monk's tales, and yet it is not quite the same. Irony, as Northrop Frye has said, is "a device which a writer uses to detach our imaginations from a world of absurdity or frustration by letting us see around it".[29] In *The Comely Cook* Čulkov seems to be using irony in this way through Martona's view of her own behavior and the experiences she has undergone. But one senses in the ironical and bantering of Ladon in the frame story and the monk in his tales that the tone is overly demeaning. It is simply an auctorial device for 'mocking' everything and everybody. In the same way as the eternal

27 *Russkaja proza XVIII veka*, p. 163.
28 *Ibid.*, p. 172.
29 Northrop Frye, *The Educated Imagination* (Bloomington, Indiana, 1964), p. 139.

burlesque references, this constant mockery can become tiresome and destructive. It does not enable the reader to 'see around absurdity and frustration', but makes it difficult for him to see them with the necessary detachment.

Martona digresses and makes generalizations about life, which show that she feels life is a matter of the survival of the fittest, that happiness is fleeting, and that you never know when fate will turn against you. She enjoys Sveton's company for about a week and says that she "would not have exchanged my lot for all the gold in the world; but, as everyone knows, happiness does not last for long and there is nothing more changeable, and so my fortune slipped and went off in quite another direction" (*fortuna moja poskol'znulas' i pošla sovsem uže drugim porjadkom*).[30]

Martona is philosophical about life's ups and downs – perhaps after the event, but would she have felt quite the same at the time or soon after? When she and Sveton are discovered by his wife near his estate and the wife slaps her and throws her out, Martona is of course unhappy, but this is how she describes the scene:

> My lover sprang up, and I jumped up. He left the room, and I suffered a dozen slaps on the face; that was just the beginning: I won't speak about the ending out of courtesy to myself. It's enough to say that pretty quickly I found myself out in the open country with no money and no companion. Then I was miserable and I really felt unhappiness: it surrounded me on all sides. But what can you do? "The bear was wrong to eat the cow, but the cow too was wrong to have wandered into the forest" (*Neprav medved', čto korovu s"el,neprava i korova, čto v les zabrela*).[31]

The final phrase does not mean that Martona does not take her situation seriously: she does. It is simply a part of her personality to avoid mawkishness and sentimentality by telling of her misfortunes in a wry and ironic manner. She quotes the famous proverb against herself for venturing away from the city into the countryside; she is essentially a city girl, and is completely lost in the country, because she relies on a rather specialized clientele.

Martona also uses proverbs to illustrate her down-to-earth attitude towards life, which at the beginning of the novel has a cynical ring. For example, very early on she tells that she knew well enough that "Wealth produces honor" (*Bogatstvo roždaet čest'*).[32] She sometimes uses proverbs with skill and humor to sum up a situation, or perhaps a

[30] *Russkaja proza XVIII veka*, p. 163.
[31] *Ibid.*, p. 165.
[32] *Ibid.*, p. 160.

character she meets. A typical application of a proverb in this manner occurs shortly after Martona has been employed as a cook in the house of the extraordinarily pious Secretary in Moscow. It will be recalled that the wife is highly promiscuous. Martona notes wrily that this woman took a fancy to her at once because "A fisherman can see another fisherman a long way off in a pool" (*Rybak rybaka daleko v plëse vidit*).[33] Martona neatly sums up the situation, the character of the woman, and her own.

Proverbs often ironize and of course the ones used in *The Comely Cook* need not be identified with Martona or her outlook. Knowing as we do Čulkov's great fondness for proverbs, which he used so often in his journal *This and That*, we are bound to feel on occasion that he has added too many of them to Martona's narrative. All that one can say about most of the proverbs is that Martona uses them effectively and that they are generally appropriately introduced.

Much the same is true of the burlesque and the Classical references that appear in the novel. Here Čulkov betrays himself a little more seriously. We have already noted that the burlesque was an inhibiting factor in his prose; clearly he has not been able to escape it entirely in this novel, although the burlesque is not very common. Even if we admit that Martona the narrator has had time to mature and acquire some culture, it is still hard to see why a woman in her position should make use of burlesque and references to Classical mythology. Possibly she picked up the habit from the soirées given by the merchant's wife. She uses burlesque oxymoron on occasion. For example, she refers to the old retired colonel who acts as her protector for a short while as 'my toothless Adonis' and later calls an old woman who is flirting with a young man at the noblewoman's house a 'toothless Grace'.[34]

The burlesque references are all used by Martona herself, except one which is used by her aged protector, the retired colonel. He is distressed when he sees a young man trying to get Martona's attention in church, and he rushes her home at once. He tells her she is very beautiful, and that unfortunately all men seem to fancy that they are like Paris; he fears he will share the same fate as Menelaus. To calm him Martona delivers an elegant speech assuring him of her complete devotion and faithfulness. Almost all the mythological references are in the high

[33] *Ibid.*, p. 166. Equivalents to the Russian proverb in English would be: "Birds of a feather flock together" or "It takes a thief to know a thief." *Plës* literally means "reach", i.e., a straight section of a river.

[34] *Russkaja proza XVIII veka*, pp. 170 and 184.

burlesque manner and are designed to emphasize Martona's beauty and its attraction to men. One night in the butler's absence, quite early in the novel before she becomes the mistress of Sveton, a man demands entrance to the house where Martona is living and bangs on the door. She is frightened: "Then I hid myself and thought that perhaps Paris had come for his Helen, for I was a (much) coveted woman (*zavidnaja ženščina*) in that city, or so I thought of myself." [35] As on a number of occasions in *The Mocker* the high burlesque is a reference to the siege of Troy. Martona is a beautiful woman and knows it; she draws a comparison between herself and Helen, but then makes fun of herself slightly for the extravagance of the comparison in the final phrase.

On another occasion during the plot with Axal' to deceive the old retired colonel, a young lad arrives to report to Martona that her sister has arrived in town from the country and will be calling to see her soon (the 'sister' will be Axal' himself disguised as a woman). Martona says that the lad was 'Mercury arrived from my Jupiter'.[36] This use of Mercury for a messenger is one of Čulkov's favorite burlesque references, but here it seems to me to be more happily applied than in *The Mocker,* and there is not quite the same mocking note of condescension.

Martona displays her skill at employing literary devices in other ways. There are at least two examples of deliberate syllepsis. After her unfortunate encounter with Sveton's wife, Martona finds herself alone in the middle of nowhere with no money but wearing an expensive silk dress. Very sensibly she decides that the luxurious dress is of no use to her and so she promptly exchanges it for a peasant dress and then sets out for Moscow having 'clothed herself with patience and the dress'.[37] A second instance of syllepsis occurs later after she has returned to the colonel's house having been tricked by Axal', who had taken for himself all the money and jewels she stole. Martona quickly sizes up the situation, sees that the colonel is distraught because she has left, and pretends it was a ruse to test his love for her. The shock of the departure has affected the man's brain and he rushes about looking for her 'having lost his wits and his glasses too'.[38]

Most of the references to Classical mythology and the proverbs occur in the early part of the novel. There may be a reason for this; it does

[35] *Russkaja proza XVIII veka*, p. 160.
[36] *Ibid.*, p. 172.
[37] *Ibid.*, p. 165.
[38] *Ibid.*, p. 177.

not seem accidental. All previous commentators on *The Comely Cook* have failed to make the point that Martona's character changes as the book proceeds: this in itself distinguishes the novel from Čulkov's previous prose fiction. Martona the heroine as presented to us by Martona the narrator begins as something of a *gamine* who is nevertheless not nearly as smart as she thinks she is. She learns quickly from the different people who cross her path and picks up some bad habits; she is at her worst when she deceives the devoted retired colonel. But Martona is then herself deceived by Axal', and immediately after her old protector's death she is thrown into prison at the instigation of the man's sister. Martona is in prison only for a brief period, but she suffers real hardship. But Axal' repents of the way he has treated Martona and arranges her release. Martona realizes that Axal' is genuinely in love with her, but she herself falls in love with his friend Svidal'. She successfully communicates to the reader the depth of her feelings for Svidal'. This is the true turning point of the novel, for Martona now begins to experience emotions to which she had earlier told us she was immune and indeed which she despised. And yet I think we have been prepared to learn that she is capable of these genuine emotions.

Axal' becomes jealous of Martona's affection for Svidal' and the two friends soon become rivals. Svidal' challenges Axal' to a duel. This is all a part of his plot to get rid of his rival, but Martona knows nothing about it. When the two rivals fight a duel, Svidal' makes sure that the pistols are not loaded and then fakes death when Axal' shoots. Axal' rushes back to Martona, tells her that he has killed Svidal' and must now leave Moscow, since dueling is against the law. Martona of course believes that Svidal' is really dead. She is grief-stricken and refuses to move, even though she risks prosecution for being involved in the duel: "Then I knew at once what the emotion of love really is. When I heard that Svidal' was dead, my blood ran cold, my throat and lips became dry, and I could hardly draw breath." [39] The ironical tone has vanished, so have the burlesque references: she is now speaking seriously about her feelings.

Although Martona does not love Axal', she is deeply touched by his fate. She receives a letter from him saying that he has been unable to overcome the pangs of remorse for killing Svidal' and that he has taken poison as the only escape from constant torment. Axal' begs Martona to visit him for one last time before he dies. Martona stays faithful to Svidal' until the end of the book at least – we cannot tell

[39] *Russkaja proza XVIII veka*, p. 181.

what might have happened in a continuation of the novel. She tells Svidal' at once about the letter from Axal'. They both decide to go to Axal' at once. Svidal' has good reason to feel guilty since by faking death he had been the direct cause of Axal' 's desperate act of suicide. Martona sees him first. When Svidal' enters the room, Axal' is terrified, believing it is the ghost of Svidal' come to torment him once more. He becomes delirious and violent, but his servant finally manages to calm him. It is at this point that the novel, or rather its first part, comes to an end.

Martona is by no means simply a counterpart of the student Neox in "The Tale of the Origin of the Taffeta Beauty Spot". It is certainly true that she is in part the typical 'vertical' heroine, for she does make her way upwards in society, going from rags to riches. But this is only a part of what happens to Martona. This would ignore the effect that Martona's experiences have upon her and the development of her character. Unlike Neox, Martona responds to the characters she meets and to her experiences. In the first half of the novel she learns from evil characters, but in the second half she begins to learn from good characters. She first feels real twinges of conscience when deceiving the old colonel, and then soon after appreciates the kindness of the repentant Axal', who tries to undo the wrong he had done her by obtaining her release from jail. She responds to the love of Svidal' and admires the generosity of the merchant who declines to seek vengeance against his noble wife for having plotted his murder. The style of the narrative as it were acts out the transformation in Martona's character. As I have already mentioned, she begins in a very lighthearted manner, quoting proverbs to illustrate her worldly-wise outlook on life, making comic burlesque references to figures of Classical mythology, using such literary devices as oxymoron and syllepsis, and commenting ironically on events and on her own role in them. However, her tone does gradually become more serious, and both proverbs and burlesque references decline in frequency – the proverbs disappear completely.

This change in tone illustrates what is probably the most important single advance made by Čulkov beyond his earlier fiction, and that is the blending of the idealistic and burlesque or comic narratives, which were kept separate in *The Mocker*. We have already seen that in isolation both types of narrative can become monotonous and that both present too one-sided a view of human life. Furthermore, we note that in this novel Čulkov did something quite unusual in the context of the state of Russian literature at that time. He took a basically 'low' theme and handled it as a subject worthy of serious literary treatment. The novel's almost tragic ending (that is, the ending of Part I) suggests that Čulkov was attempting to raise the level of prose fiction to that enjoyed by tragedy. There was significantly a similar cross-fertilization of genres in France during the seventeenth century, when Madame de Lafayette introduced the theme of tragic love to the novel having learned a great deal from earlier French neo-Classical tragedy.[40] In fact Èmin had tried to do something quite similar a few years before Čulkov's novel appeared. He borrowed certain themes and even parts of whole speeches from the tragedies of the French dramatists of the previous century, including Corneille's *Le Cid*. However, these borrowings are completely swallowed up in the morass of extraordinary shipwrecks and numerous other adventures, and so lose whatever effect they might have had. Furthermore, Èmin's heroes are all supermen and his heroines models of virtue and patience: they are cardboard figures, quite unlike Martona and her two lovers Axal' and Svidal'. Èmin's novels, like Čulkov's own collection of tales *The Mocker*, are very strong in events, but woefully weak in characterization: the characters for the most part simply act, they never change or develop.

The social distinctions, the distinctions between high and low characters that had been carefully observed in the tales of *The Mocker*, are now broken down in *The Comely Cook*. With Martona, a sergeant's widow, as the focal point, we also find in the novel a wealthy nobleman Sveton, a colonel, other nobles of varying degrees, a Secretary, a butler, a merchant, and so on. But we do not find any kings or princes; Čulkov has moved down the social scale and then introduced characters of a quite broad social spectrum. The 'high' characters are not necessarily noble and good, and the 'low' characters are not necessarily scurvy knaves. In one instance at least, a member of the merchant class is shown to have a more generous and honorable nature than his noble wife.

We have also seen the stylistic stratification break down in this novel. In *The Mocker* a relatively lofty and staid style is used by Ladon (of course, not in the frame story), while the monk uses a much more colloquial and even on occasion vulgar style for his tales. We no longer find a high style of narration reserved for 'high' events and a low style for 'low' events, since a more uniform narrative tone is maintained by Martona, although it does become increasingly serious as the novel

[40] See: F. C. Green, *French Novelists, Manners and Ideas* (New York, 1929), p. 46.

proceeds. There are occasional switches in style which are specially motivated. When the old colonel finds that Martona has returned after leaving him the previous night (she had planned to elope with Axal', but he had abandoned her), he expresses both his joy and his distraught condition in the following manner:

Is it but a dream that is tempting me with this pleasant vision, is it but a flattering hope that is deceiving my reason? Beautiful Martona! Is it really you that I am holding in my arms, are these your lips that I am kissing now, are these your charms which I see? Is it you here before me? Speak, answer, my darling, or have I already lost you forever?[41]

These rather banal rhetorical questions seem to fit the old colonel well and also serve to make him a more pathetic figure.

There is a considerable amount of dialogue in the novel, or rather direct quoted speech, which is perhaps unexpected in a first-person narrative. In having characters differentiated by their speech and in having them speak more naturally instead of delivering enormously long perorations, Čulkov was making a startling innovation in prose fiction. At the beginning of the novel the butler discovers that Martona has received a gift from another man. He is naturally angry and tells her that he is going to make her pay for her infidelity:

Until now I thought that I was the only one who knew you, but now I see that every man in town is visiting you one after the other. I am going to show you right now what a splendid lady you are. I am going now and when I have brought back the horses, I'll strip you of every last thing (I gave you). Go live off somebody else, and give me back everything of mine, every single thing.[42]

Martona's aristocratic lovers never speak to her so roughly as that, and they never use the familiar singular *ty* form of address. This is how Axal' bids farewell to Martona after he believes he has shot and killed Svidal' in a duel:

Dear madam! Not concerned with your situation, I loved you with all my heart. My own faults were the reason for my deceiving you, but having left you, I realized that I could never be happy without you. So I returned to Moscow and when I learned that you were in prison, I did all in my power to help you, and I managed to do so. Finally, I resolved to fulfill the promise I had given you and I returned to marry you. But merciless fate is depriving me of that happiness; at this very moment I must leave Moscow

[41] *Russkaja proza XVIII veka*, p. 177.
[42] *Ibid.*, p. 161.

and Russia too. I am a wretched man and am now suffering cruel torture. Farewell, my darling, forever – I have shot Svidal'.[43]

To some degree Čulkov was as limited by literary tradition as was Èmin before him. It is clear that dialogue entered prose fiction first more successfully where 'low' characters were involved. In confrontations of 'high' or noble characters, Čulkov had a tendency to borrow from the tragedians. Nevertheless, the noble characters in *The Comely Cook* do speak with much greater brevity and less ponderously than the heroes of tragedy. The speeches and letters of the aristocratic lovers are, after all, being filtered through the narrative style of Martona.

Although the monk's long tale, "The Tale of the Origin of the Taffeta Beauty Spot", is not nearly so episodic and amorphous as Ladon's narrative in *The Mocker*, it bears no comparison to the novel in its careful structural organization. *The Comely Cook* in fact pivots on Martona's relationship with the old retired colonel, since it is at that point that she begins to feel real sympathy for another person and guilt at her own behavior. Furthermore, it is during her stay with the colonel that she meets Axal' and a train of events are set in motion, which culminate in the suicide and gradually take on a tragic coloring. The excellent structuring of the novel indeed points up the need for a continuation. It was a good idea to end the first part of the novel at the point where Axal' is dying of poison, since the reader is anxious to go on to the second part and learn what took place next. The reader is bound to be concerned with the possible effect of his death on Martona and Svidal', both of whom seem to be so deeply affected by what has happened to him. Axal' has used the money and jewels he had taken from Martona to buy an estate, and this fact is a good illustration of the way episodes in the novel are knit together. Axal' gives the deed of the estate to Martona in remorse for the way he had treated her earlier. But this adds a further complication because, since Martona now has the deed to an estate and its serfs, she is a woman of independent means. Although Martona seems to be in love with Svidal', this might have its effect upon her relationship with him. Šklovskij, in his monograph on *Čulkov and Levšin*, suggests that the novel is really complete and argues that in any case one can never bring a first-person narrative to an end. Surely, this is Šklovskij being too clever by half. One can imagine any number of ways in which a writer might complete a first-person narrative in a satisfactory manner.

[43] *Ibid.*, p. 181.

It is instructive to see what Čulkov did not borrow from *The Mocker* as well as how he combined the various elements that he did. Čulkov naturally had to abandon the magical features of Ladon's tales; there are no sudden transformations of man into animal or tree. The transformations that do occur are of a quite different nature. For example, when Martona changes lovers at the beginning of the novel from butler to the butler's master Sveton, she is amazed to see that with a noble protector she no longer has anything to fear, and her anxiety changes to happiness. The 'transformation' (*prevaščenie*) in her fortunes, she tells us, was a great surprise to her.

Naturally, *The Comely Cook* does not contain any lengthy journeys studded with fantastic adventures; Martona's journey from Kiev to the countryside to stay near Sveton's estate is not at all the same as those in Ladon's narrative. What Čulkov did take over from Ladon's narrative, he adapted and modernized. In the novel the supposed death of a hero now takes on a new meaning for the structure of the total work, and also has its direct causes in human motivation: Svidal' fakes death in his duel with Axal' so as to get rid of a troublesome rival. This episode is made to work because we learn something about Martona from her reactions to the supposed death of Svidal'.

In *The Comely Cook* we find a very brief interpolated story, but it has a direct link with the main plot line of the novel. Svidal' instructs a servant to tell a story to a gathering of guests at the house of the merchant in such a way as to reveal to the merchant the true nature of his noble wife and her responsibility for the plot that nearly resulted in his death. The familiar dressing of the hero in woman's clothing is also used in the novel when Axal' pretends to be Martona's sister visiting from the provinces, but here again the traditional technique is well integrated into the plot.[44] It is an amusing scene and the episode is told with verve and wit. Before her 'sister' arrives, Martona tells the old colonel that she is very beautiful and admonishes him that he must take care not to fall in love with her. Finally Axal' arrives in disguise and the two sisters hug and kiss each other to demonstrate their great affection; they are supposed to be seeing each other for the first time in five years. The trusting colonel looks on benignly at these signs of fondness

[44] The technique has of course been used in most European literatures and has been canonized for English literature since Shakespeare used it so often. There is a possible echo of this episode in Puškin's poem "Domik v Kolomne" ("The Little House in Kolomna"), in which a suitor obtains entrance to the household by pretending to be a woman cook named Mavruša. The poem ends when mother returns early from church and discovers the cook shaving!

and expresses pleasure at seeing members of the same family staying so close together even though they are poor.

There is also in the novel a more effective use of the 'commercial motif', to which reference was made in Chapter I. This is how Martona relates one of her early agreements with a certain gentleman:

> Our first rendezvous was a business meeting, and we spoke of nothing except drawing up a contract. He bargained for my charms and I offered them to him for a respectable price; then we signed receipts in order to seal the agreement, of which the middle-man was love and my landlady [that is, the procuress] was the witness.[45]

An instance of a different use of this motif occurs later in the novel when Martona falls in love with Svidal'. As though to contrast her relationship with him to the commercial relationships she had earlier had with other men, Martona says that she and Svidal' loved 'without any bargaining' (*bez vsjakogo torgu*).[46] We accept this as the truth – Martona experiences an emotion which takes possession of her to such an extent that all financial matters are banished from her thoughts. And yet we would find it difficult to believe that this could be anything but a temporary state of mind. We know that Martona has fallen in love with Svidal', but at the same time we recall that Martona has been forced to learn the facts of life the hard way: it is inconceivable that she would lose all thought of the precariousness of her position and simply live from day to day with no concern for the future. Consequently, it is no surprise to find her a short while afterwards outlining for her reader, seemingly with a certain amount of satisfaction at the generosity of Svidal' who is thus showing his great affection for her, the elaborate financial arrangements that are to govern their very happy but illicit relationship. She even permits herself a certain gaiety:

> Thus, in order to strengthen our mutual love, he decided to give me an annual salary of two thousand rubles, not including gifts and my other caprices. In addition, he promised to give me a thousand rubles if I gave birth to a child and it looked like him. And then I began to pray, forgetting for the moment that heaven is not obliged to bless our sins. . . .[47]

However, Martona goes on to say at once: "This wealth afforded me little joy, for I had already seen enough of it; but I resolved to be a little more careful and determined to set aside something for a rainy day."

[45] *Russkaja proza XVIII veka*, p. 161.
[46] *Ibid.*, p. 181.
[47] *Ibid.*, p. 183.

As in Ladon's narrative, there are in this novel references to Fate and its inconstancy, but they seem to have more point and also serve to characterize the users. When Martona complains that one can never tell what tricks Fate will play, then the reader will readily agree with her and see the justice of her remarks, for throughout most of the novel she is in a precarious position. By the time she meets and falls in love with Svidal', Martona has realized that life has its ups and downs, and one simply has to try to do something about it. Axal' too complains of Fate's waywardness in much the same way as do Ladon's heroes, but his complaints are linked quite clearly with the torments he feels because of his supposed crime of killing Svidal' in the duel. Like his nightmares (the same is true of the colonel's nightmares), the complaints of Axal' reveal his psychological state and transform him into a hero of tragedy, although it is true that the story does have melodramatic features.

There is of course dramatic irony in the fact that Axal' is tormenting himself for a crime that he did not commit. A further example of the increased sophistication in the novel occurs when Axal' rushes back to Martona from his duel and tells her that he has killed Svidal'. We have quoted the passage in which Axal' explains that he most now leave the city at once. Martona faints. In a nice touch Martona adds that Axal' left her "with many tears and much grief, believing that I had fainted at the thought of parting with him".[48] She had of course fainted at the news of the death of Svidal', whom she already loved far more than Axal'. Another illustration of this misunderstanding of motives by a character in the novel occurs a little earlier after Martona has returned to the colonel's house from her unsuccessful rendezvous with Axal'. As soon as she enters the house, the colonel's steward gives her a hard slap on the face. Martona rushes at once to see the colonel and pretends she was testing his love by leaving him. He bursts into tears of gratitude for her return. Martona says that she too cried: "I embraced him quite sincerely and shed tears which had already been prepared for me by the steward's slap." [49]

No other character in the novel can match Martona for complexity; quite obviously the reader learns far more about her than about the other characters, who are shown only externally. However, Axal' is a character of great interest. He too has a certain complexity and is neither a mindless rogue like Neox nor a superhuman hero like Alim

[48] *Russkaja proza XVIII veka*, p. 181.
[49] *Ibid.*, p. 177.

or Kidal in Ladon's narrative. He begins as a typical amorous rogue, disguising himself as a girl in order to develop a liaison with Martona, offering to elope with her and then abandoning her. However, it is this same Axal' who shows Martona the first real kindness she experiences in the novel – an act of kindness based solely on his love for her and the regret he felt for the shabby way in which he had behaved. This act and his jealousy of Svidal' are the two main external demonstrations of his feelings for Martona that she passes along to the reader. A further very significant fact that illustrates the part she plays in his life is his writing to her on his death bed and begging her to come and visit him before he dies.

In this novel Čulkov has shown considerable development as a writer of prose fiction. From a purely literary standpoint it is the most satisfying of his works for the modern reader. *The Comely Cook* can be read entirely on its own terms, something that cannot be said for too many works, either in prose or verse, written in the eighteenth century in Russia. In this chapter I have tried to show the progress made by Čulkov towards greater depth of characterization, increased psychological finesse, more human motivation, and a more realistic background. I have also tried to show how this novel forms the culminating point of Čulkov's development as a prose writer, and that in it certain problems which were discerned in his earlier works find an acceptable solution. The crucial change is the choice of a complex character as a first-person narrator, who tells us about her own adventures, not a series of tales about the adventures of others. Also vitally important is the switch to contemporary Russia for the novel's setting. Čulkov managed finally to escape the dichotomy of styles and narrative manners which resulted largely from the fact of his having two broad traditions of narrative prose upon which to draw, but also in part reflected the effect of the Russian classicist *Weltanschauung* upon him and his work.

The possibilities for prose fiction opened up by Čulkov with his novel *The Comely Cook* were considerable, and yet they were not explored by many of his contemporaries. Nevertheless, Čulkov's was a remarkable achievement. The native printed tradition in prose fiction was almost negligible in Russia at that time. Čulkov did borrow some features from the slightly earlier novels, or rather romances, of Fëdor Èmin, but for the most part they served him rather as objects of satire and parody. The influence of the Russian manuscript tales on the novel appears to be only peripheral. Once again, as with Čulkov's previous prose, it is easier to link him with Western European writers than with any predecessor in his own country. In the case of *The Comely Cook*, however, we are more likely to compare him to writers of the first half of the eighteenth century than with French writers of the first half of the seventeenth century, as was the case with his earlier work *The Mocker*.[50]

In the eighteenth century Russian literature underwent an extremely rapid period of development and absorbed diverse influences from many sources. The novel genre is a case in point. Quite suddenly in the middle of the eighteenth century Russians had available to them in translation novels of almost every conceivable description. The rise of the native Russian novel is consequently chaotic and rapid. Čulkov provides us with an excellent example of the telescoped nature of literary developments at that time in Russia. In the space of four short years, from 1766 to 1770 when *The Comely Cook* appeared, it is almost as though Čulkov proceeded through several stages in the development of the novel which in France and England had lasted for more than a century. Namely, the development that took place in the novel from the *Astré* of Honoré d'Urfé to the post-picaresque *Moll Flanders* of Daniel Defoe, or to Prévost's *Manon Lescaut*, for Martona is very similar to Manon in a number of ways.[51]

In many ways Čulkov's situation is predominantly neo-classical environment closely resembled that of Scarron in France over a century before. In spite of their differences, the two men played a somewhat similar role historically, and one might well say of Čulkov's *The Comely Cook* what has been said of Scarron's *Le roman comique*:

[It] is no small performance, and historically it is almost great. We have in it, indeed, got entirely out of the pure romance; but we have also got out of the *fatrasie* – the mingle-mangle of story, jargon, nonsense, and what not, – out of the mere tale of adventure, out of the mere tale of *grivoiserie*. We have borrowed the comic dramatist's mirror – the "Muses' Looking-

[50] The influence of Scarron is felt in Čulkov's parodical introduction to *The Comely Cook*. He dedicates it to a highly placed patron, but says he will not name him because he fears people will associate him with the contents of the novel. Scarron wrote a similar parodical dedication to *Le roman comique*.

[51] *Manon Lescaut* was not made available in Russian until 1790, when the final part of Prévost's *Mémoires d'un homme de qualité qui s'est retiré du monde* was finally translated. A translation of the earlier parts of the novel had begun to appear much earlier in 1756! Andrej Bolotov tells us that he even took to learning French so as to be able to finish the novel.

glass" – and are holding it up to nature without the intervention of the conventionalities of the stage.[52]

In fact, with *The Comely Cook* Čulkov has moved beyond Scarron's novel, which has more in common with *The Mocker*. As we have said, it seems more appropriate to link *The Comely Cook* with the type of fiction being produced in France and England in the first half of the eighteenth century rather than with that of a hundred years earlier. What Čulkov did with this novel was to introduce the autobiographical form into Russian literature. Speaking of the introduction of the autobiographical form into French literature, Vivienne Mylne notes that it "entailed two major developments: since the stories were modern, it no longer seemed appropriate to endow characters with the perfections attributed to personnages of a remote and heroic past; and since the narrator was telling his own life-story, he could give a full account of his own motives and reactions. The memoir-novel, in other words, opened the door to realistic and detailed character-portrayal."[53] What is true of French literature also holds for Russian literature; it gives one a fair measure of Čulkov's achievement.

[52] George Saintsbury, *A History of the French Novel*, I (London, 1917), p. 280.
[53] Vivienne Mylne, "Sensibility and the Novel", in *French Literature and Its Background*, ed. John Cruickshank (Oxford, 1968), p. 45.

VI

FRIEND OF THE MUSES

Čulkov may be said to have abandoned literature proper after the publication of *The Comely Cook* in 1770. I have already speculated as to his reasons and suggested that in all probability the chief factor in his decision was the lack of a broadly based reading public sufficiently interested and affluent to buy his works of original verse and prose fiction. The years 1770 to 1774 saw the publication of his *Collection of Various Songs* in four volumes, but the rest of Čulkov's life was devoted to his career as a bureaucrat or to the writing of non-literary works, notably his *Historical Description of Russian Commerce,* which seems to have occupied most of his time during the eighties.

Significantly, it was only towards the end of his life, when his financial situation was fully secured, that he returned to literature. After a period of twenty years Čulkov added a fifth part to his collection of tales *The Mocker* when a third edition of the work appeared in 1789. Since this fifth part did not appear in the second edition of 1783-1784, we can assume that the material in it was written some time shortly before 1789. For the most part Čulkov has maintained the overall tone of Ladon's narrative, but certain new features are nonetheless apparent. The realistic elements which we have noted in Čulkov's earlier work are more pronounced in some tales of the fifth part. At the same time we note that Čulkov became more conservative in his last years and abandoned his former belief that literature could not affect morals and manners. This in its turn further increased the realistic element in his work because he engaged in social satire, something which he does only rarely at the beginning of his career.

Čulkov became a landowner in 1783 and, as we saw in our first chapter, in 1785 he composed on his new estate his "Instruction to My Young Son About to Enter Service", which was not published until 1790 in the second edition of his *Economic Notes*. In the list of seven works which he commends to the attention of his son for careful study we can certainly discern a change in literary attitudes, a sort of literary conservatism.[1] If we recall the numerous occasions on which Čulkov stated in categorical terms that he felt literature had no moral effect, or satirized those who thought it did, then we are bound to be surprised at some of the items on the list.[2] To illustrate: Marmontel's *Bélisaire* is an extreme – one might almost say notorious – example of the didactic novel. This is precisely the type of work that Čulkov would earlier have abhorred or ridiculed. Clearly we have here a radical change in outlook, but we do not really know how or why it came about. We can speculate on the possible influence that his association with Aleksandr Radiščev had upon him while they were working together at the Commerce Department: Čulkov began working there in 1772, Radiščev in 1777.

Another book in Čulkov's list was Rousseau's *Discours sur les sciences et les arts*. This work was written by Rousseau in 1750 and was designed to prove the thesis that the 'noble savage' is superior to civilized man. The influence of this work on Čulkov is corroborated by an episode in Ladon's narrative in the fifth part of *The Mocker*. One of the heroes named Kidal has a dream, during which he is taken by a giant bird called Rok to another planet: later we are told this is the moon. Kidal finds that on the moon people and wild animals live together in harmony. The people are living in a sort of Golden Age. They find Kidal and his clothing strange, but treat him hospitably and permit him to go freely everywhere and examine their society. The inhabitants, as Kidal soon learns, are not in the least interested in science; they are very religious, philosophical and concerned especially with ethical and moral problems. They live without laws of any kind; they have no money, and no inventors; they have a produce economy of a primitive type.[3] The narrator portrays this lunar utopia in favorable terms and it seems very likely that Čulkov himself had come to regard such an existence as ideal. There is nothing like this in the earlier parts of *The Mocker* or anywhere else in his earlier work. There can be little doubt that Čulkov borrowed the features of his lunar utopia from Rousseau. It is indeed strange, given his earlier work, to find Čulkov engaging in the creation of utopias.[4]

[1] *Ekonomičeskie zapiski* (Moscow, 1790).
[2] The list is quoted in full in Chapter I, p. 35.
[3] *Peresmešnik*, V, 27-52.
[4] Cf. the utopias of Ščerbatov, and Radiščev in his *Putešestvie iz Peterburga v Moskvu*.

We also note changes in the narrative tone of the monk's tales, particularly in "The Tale of the Origin of the Taffeta Beauty Spot", which is brought to a conclusion in the fifth part of *The Mocker*. Only a feeble attempt is made to maintain the undercutting and ironical narrative tone that was so much a feature of the earlier sections of this tale. Asides from the narrator are almost totally absent. Neox too is made as respectable as possible in the circumstances. At once he becomes private secretary to a very important person and hence has no need to remain the gigolo of the merchant's wife: she immediately finds another lover. Čulkov also quickly dissociates Neox from the other disreputable female in his life, Vladimira. It seems that she has arrived in Vineta but is to marry a noble of the town.

A beautiful young woman invites Neox to a rendezvous but mysteriously refuses to reveal her identity. She gives him money. So far the episode seems to be a repetition of his encounters with Vladimira. However, there are important differences. Although the lady's father is a corrupt noble, there is no suggestion of doing away with him. Neox is now very successful at court and even on intimate terms with the king of Vineta. It is the king's idea to have Neox mark the woman's cheek at one of their assignations so that she will be easy to single out at a ball the king holds for precisely that purpose. The king then ordains that Neox and his lady shall be married. From this outline it is clear that the 'roguish' and amoral nature of Neox and of those with whom he associates has been pushed into the background by Čulkov, who by the eighties no longer found it appropriate to write about such base and ignoble creatures as had appeared in the earlier parts of the tale.

The changes that had taken place in Čulkov's outlook during the seventies and eighties and the effects they had on his writing are nowhere more apparent than in the three short stories that bring the fifth and final part of *The Mocker* to a close. There is no indication as to the narrator; by this time Čulkov had really abandoned the fiction of the oral narrative established in the frame story. The stories seem to be narrated by a different type of narrator from the one whom we have seen before. All three stories are set in provincial Russia in Čulkov's own times.

In the first story, "A Bitter Fate" ("Gor'kaja učast' "), a poor peasant Sysoj Fofanov is sent into the army by wealthy peasants. He is demobilized when he loses a hand in battle, and returns home. The narrator says that Fofanov's journey back home was not so glorious or notable as those of Prince Bova or Peter of the Golden Keys, and he will pass over it in silence. This a strong piece of literary and social satire. The Russian manuscript tales are here used as a foil by being ignored or regarded as inappropriate; Čulkov does not parody them or make fun of their romantic settings and heroic adventures, but stresses the wretchedness and misery that surround a peasant soldier returning from war to his village in 'real life'. The pull towards realism, quite apparent here and elsewhere in the stories, is strengthened by such social satire.

When Fofanov returns to his village, he finds his whole family – his mother, father, small brother, and sister – all dead in very peculiar circumstances. Finally, we learn what had happened. The small sister had stabbed her baby brother while sleep-walking, then in terror hid in the stove. The following morning the mother had got up and lit the stove without looking in, thus burning the girl to death. Later the father had discovered that both his children were dead and at once killed his wife in rage. But then he was overcome with remorse and hanged himself.

The story is related with the utmost seriousness and the narrator makes no bones about displaying overt sympathy for the peasants and pity for their hard lot. It is a pro-peasant work and the narrator states at the outset:

> Envy and hatred are exactly the same among peasants as they are among city dwellers; but since peasants are purer than the inhabitants of towns, these vices are more readily noticeable in them than in the refined, smooth-mannered people (*politiki*) living at court and in the city.[5]

The rather extraordinary events linked with the solemn and pro-peasant tone remind us of Radiščev's *Journey from St. Petersburg to Moscow,* which appeared in early 1790, only a few months after the fifth part of *The Mocker* was published. The possibility of direct influence, not of Radiščev's book perhaps, although the manuscript was largely completed in 1788, but of his views on the social structure of Russia and the natural superiority of peasants to the corrupt urban dwellers cannot be excluded. Čulkov seems to have taken over the idea of the 'noble savage' and linked it to the Russian peasant, who then becomes the 'natural man'. There is a striking difference between the favorable treatment of peasants in this story and Čulkov's earlier works, particu-

[5] *Russkaja proza XVIII veka*, p. 146.

larly the tales told by the monk, in which peasants are portrayed simply as foolish louts. One might say that in his changing attitude towards the peasant Čulkov was taking part in the late eighteenth-century sentimentalist movement in Russia, which adopted a somewhat similar stance.

The social satire in the story is new in Čulkov's prose fiction and may owe something to the influence of Radiščev and also of Nikolaj Novikov, with whom Čulkov had crossed pens in 1769. At that time Čulkov had declined to follow Novikov in producing social satire in his journal, but he does use it in this story. When the death of Fofanov's family is reported to the nearest town, the local officials take six weeks before even beginning their investigation into the mysterious tragedy. After a cursory examination of the situation, an official decides that the peasant killed all the members of his family while drunk and then fell over and struck his head (the father had in fact hanged himself). The case is closed. "Some people", never identified, investigate further and discover the truth. Once again, one notes the satire directed against inefficient and stupid officials, who have such a low opinion of peasants and pay no attention to the obvious facts in the case. Fofanov spends whatever money he has to bury his family and then is left to face the future without hope.

The other two stories are also set in contemporary Russia and contain a good deal of implied criticism of social ills. The first is entitled "Gingerbread Money" ("Prjaničnaja moneta"). It is a moral tale about a retired major who loves nothing but money. The narrative tone once more is rather solemn, and one could say that the story illustrates the final stage of Čulkov's developing serious attitude towards Russian reality. However, in the first story and partly in this second story the serious attitude tends to get rather close to that with which Čulkov approached the characters and events in Ladon's narrative. We can see that he was not able, or did not care, to maintain the appropriate narrative distance in both instances.

In this story about the retired major the narrator warns his reader soberly right at the outset: "True human wealth is reason and virtue, and true poverty is the lack of these gifts." [6] This sounds like a sentence from Čulkov's "Instruction" to his son. It may have been easier for him to take this detached view of wealth and poverty when he was fairly well established in government service and owned some property. This was not quite the way he looked at such matters in his earlier works.

[6] *Russkaja proza XVIII veka*, p. 150.

Here what we have called the commercial motif finds a somewhat different application from those illustrated at the beginning of this study. Čulkov mentions the illegal selling of wine carried on by unscrupulous men, and also the get-rich-quick tax-farmers, but cautiously adds that such abuses and such men USED to exist in Russia; now they are exceptions. Major Fufaev is such an exception. He engages in the illegal selling of wine. Instead of having the peasants come to his house and pay money for the wine, he has them buy gingerbread cookies and cakes at certain fixed prices from his agents in the local village. The peasants then come to his house and present these cookies and cakes in order to receive the appropriate measure of wine. The major gets rich very quickly because he deals fairly and is widely respected. He dies in his bed, unpunished and unrepentant. Čulkov does not round his story off with a moral, nor does he have it end 'happily' with the arrest of the major.

The final story is entitled "The Precious Pike" ("Dragocennaja ščuka"). Its theme resembles that of the previous story, but it differs from both it and the first story chiefly because of its ironical narrative tone. This tone is, however, not obtrusive and there are no auctorial digressions. Čulkov has managed to introduce a moral voice into the narrative with considerable subtlety; narrative distance is maintained throughout, although the social satire is clearly present.

In the story a retired court councillor is appointed governor, or *voevoda*, of a certain provincial town. When the local merchants and officials present him with lavish gifts as bribes, as though they were calling cards, the new governor much to everyone's amazement and consternation warns them sternly against such behavior. The merchants and officials, like those in the comedy *The Government Inspector* (*Revizor*) by Gogol', are completely bewildered by the new man who is to rule over the town. What are they to do with a man who will not accept bribes? The governor is simply not playing the game according to the established rules. The merchants and officials bustle and fluster like those in Gogol's play, trying to think of ways in which they can bribe the new governor and fearing lest they offend him again and get themselves into real hot water. The delightful thing about the whole situation is that the officials simply cannot conceive of a governor who does not accept bribes: they are by no means put off by the new governor's apparent moral scruples. There is of course no need for Čulkov to make the point laboriously in an aside.

The desperate officials finally turn for advice to a wise old man of the town, who suggests that they try to find out if the new governor has any special likes. They sigh with relief when they discover that he is inordinately fond of pike: the problem is solved, for this is the clue they have been seeking. They are not in the least disturbed to find that they must buy pike from the governor's own fishmonger when they wish to make him a gift of his favorite dish. For a single pike they have to pay large sums, commensurate always with the importance of the favors they seek from the governor. Once again life settles down to the familiar corrupt routine in which everyone knows he must pay for any favor the governor does him. After five years the governor leaves the town and at a farewell banquet (at which the pike are naturally supplied by the local merchants) he justifies his behavior with the utmost frankness. Everyone seems to be perfectly content with corruption as a way of life and would be puzzled in earnest by an official who meant what he said and refused to accept bribes in any shape or form. At the end of the story the governor departs after his tour of duty in the provincial town, honored and regretted by all.

This final tale is brief and pointed in its social satire and nothing is out of place. It shows that Čulkov was capable of writing excellent satire, which has a nineteenth-century ring about it. I have mentioned Gogol'; one also thinks of Saltykov-Ščedrin's tales directed against corrupt officials in provincial Russia. The story is quite remarkable for its satirical understatement: it is satirical because it is amusing, but is amusing to a purpose. In one important respect it seems more 'modern' to the present-day reader than does the novel *The Comely Cook*. This story contains no burlesque references whatsoever, neither high nor low, neither to the mythological figures of Classical antiquity nor to the Slavic pagan gods and goddesses. This, it seems to me, is a significant advance over Čulkov's earlier works, although one must remember that it came after a gap of some fifteen to twenty years in his development. The story can therefore be regarded as the culminating point in Čulkov's progress towards the realistic manner of narration. In it he adopts the ironical tone which is typical of his best manner, but withdraws from the action more than he had done previously, except in *The Comely Cook*; but the novel is something of a special case because it is a first-person narrative. Čulkov writes about the lower and middle classes in the Russia of his own day, and does not try to write about kings and queens in a setting with which he was quite unfamiliar. He neither denigrates his material, nor does he attempt to elevate it with high burlesque; he simply accepts it. This of course does not mean that

Čulkov displays no angle of vision – as I have said, his tone is ironical and a moral voice is present in the story.

Čulkov's sympathetic treatment of the peasant on the one hand, and his satire directed at corrupt provincial officials on the other were both significant trends in the literature of the period, but at the same time presaged very important and fruitful motifs that were not fully exploited by Russian writers until the first half of the nineteenth century. One could argue of course that in terms of Čulkov's own development his use of social satire was a retrogressive step; it would have been more interesting had he sought to pursue the possibilities of the memoir-novel. Socially and politically Čulkov might have been progressive in following the lead of Novikov and Radiščev, but he was conservative in literary terms. It is curious too that when he was poor, Čulkov declined to use literature as a means of attacking social injustice, and yet when he had become a landowner he was prepared to do so.

Some of Čulkov's contemporaries thought of him as a cynical opportunist, who produced whatever the public wanted. At the beginning of this century V. V. Sipovskij accused him of lacking seriousness: "He called his own works 'rubbish' – perhaps because he was too imbued with skepticism – and he would not subject himself to any literary laws or aims. . . ." [7] Russian scholars have found Čulkov difficult to categorize, to place in the general history of Russian literature during the reign of Catherine II. During the Soviet period we find Viktor Šklovskij commenting: "Mixajlo Čulkov was a writer outside any group. Rather he failed to create one." [8] More recently, in an article which discusses the uses and aims of the term 'literary movement', A. N. Sokolov makes the remark: "One also meets in literary history 'anonymous' movements, which received no title in their time (for example, the works of the democratic writers in Russian literature of the eighteenth century, Čulkov, Popov, Levšin, and others." [9]

Had Čulkov's career as a writer of prose fiction not been interrupted after 1770, I have no doubt that scholars would have agreed that the early idealized narrative of Ladon was merely a part of his literary apprenticeship. Certainly he might have continued Ladon's narrative in a fifth part of *The Mocker*, as he did in fact do much later in 1789,

[7] *Očerki po istorii russkogo romana* (St. Petersburg, 1909), p. 588.

[8] *Čulkov i Levšin* (Leningrad, 1933), p. 79.

[9] A. N. Sokolov, "Literaturnoe napravlenie (Opyt stat'i dlja terminologičeskogo slovarja)", *Izvestija Ak. Nauk SSSR. Otd. lit. i jazyka*, XXI (1962), No. 5, 410. By referring to Čulkov and others as *demokratičeskie literatory*, Sokolov tends to beg the question.

but I have tried to show that in the years 1769 and 1770 Čulkov was beginning to move away from the romance or idealized manner of narrative towards the more down-to-earth anti-romance and even towards what I have called a realistic manner; this latter trend does not find full development until 1789 in the final three tales of Part V of *The Mocker*. It seems hardly surprising that as a young man Čulkov, like preceding generations of French and English readers, was impressed by the French seventeenth-century romances and sought to try his hand at this type of fiction. He may well have been influenced by the enormous success of Èmin's works in the same manner.

As we have seen, Čulkov was also very much impressed by Scarron's burlesque anti-romance and borrowed from it in large measure for the ironical narrative tone employed in the frame story and in the monk's tales. In the early part of his career Čulkov was therefore borrowing from the two major narrative prose traditions of the time. His case is unusual because he was not parodying the works of other authors (with the possible exception of Èmin), but his own. This provides an excellent illustration of his isolation and lack of predecessors in his own country, and also of the telescoped and jumbled nature of literary trends during this period.

The dichotomy between romance and anti-romance in Čulkov's work, and in part the further dichotomy of his non-noble background and his neo-classical education, created certain problems since they affected his attitude towards his material and towards Russian reality as a subject for literature. The crucial problem was that Čulkov approached with seriousness only the ideal and unreal world of Ladon's narrative. He adopted a bantering, ironical attitude when writing about the more recognizable, 'real' world that is pictured in the monk's tales. This unwillingness, or perhaps at first inability, to approach Russian reality with seriousness, or at least to take it as worthy of sober and thoughtful attention, was a particularly important impediment to Čulkov's development, since historically modern prose fiction has drawn its material from the real world and sought to create the illusion of reality. Čulkov's extensive use of the mock heroic or high burlesque is a further case in point; by this use of the burlesque in relation to characters and events set more obviously in the real world of his time, Čulkov revealed the strong Russian neo-classical tendency to satirize reality or attempt to 'elevate' it, as though it had no right to an independent literary existence of its own.

In his novel *The Comely Cook* the burlesque references are few in number, and those that are present operate in a somewhat different way than those in the monk's tales; their purpose is not to elevate or ridicule low characters and events, but to help characterize the narrator Martona. The abandonment of the burlesque, or its curtailment and modification, did not mean that Čulkov abandoned the ironical narrative manner. Indeed, this manner shows him at his most natural and successful. What happened essentially was that Čulkov finally managed to avoid too much auctorial intrusion into the narrative – the fault of both the idealistic and burlesque traditions which seemed to hinder him most. In his best work the ironical tone is present, but the author maintains the appropriate narrative distance.

Linked with the question of ironical tone and narrative distance is that of the purpose of literature. Čulkov was opposed to the central neo-classical dogma of the moral purpose of literature, or rather he was opposed to the manifestations in literary works of the dogma. Čulkov took the relatively sophisticated attitude that overt moralizing by an author should be avoided. As we have seen, a little later in life Čulkov came to change his mind on this matter and even recommended moralizing works to his son for his edification. And in his later stories there was a tendency for him to point the direction rather obviously for his reader. However, Čulkov does in his own practice avoid overt moralizing or openly stating the message that his reader is supposed to take away with him from the stories.

Although in many ways Russian literature during the reign of the Empress Catherine offers us a picture of bewildering and sometimes chaotic development it was generally a period when an attempt was made to uphold some if not all of the tenets of neo-classicism. Čulkov as a writer of prose fiction did not fit readily into the framework created by these tenets. Čulkov does, as some scholars have pointed out, appear as an isolated figure. He had no predecessors, with the very minor exception of Èmin, and no immediate followers, with the exception of Vasilij Levšin, who emulated Čulkov's 'Slavic tales' in his own *Russian Tales* (*Russkie skazki*).

If Čulkov himself did not pursue the new directions he had indicated, particularly with his novel *The Comely Cook*, we cannot be surprised that no one else did. After the Pugačëv Rebellion, which was crushed in 1775, and more noticeably in the eighties, the literary atmosphere changed, as is evident from some sections of the fifth part of *The Mocker,* and a sentimentalist strain began to become apparent in Russian literature. A new generation of readers had new tastes and there seemed little room for Čulkov's subject matter and ironical narrative tone. It was not really until many years later, with the works of Gogol' (and partly of Narežnyj a little earlier), that we see a continuation of the tradition initiated by Čulkov. He himself did no have an opportunity to resume his literary interests because he died in 1792 at the age of forty-nine.

The Institute of Russian Literature in Leningrad possesses a bronze plaque with a portrait of Čulkov, and underneath it the following epitaph:

> Whom does this sad monument cover;
> Alas, the ashes of Čulkov rest beneath it,
> Čulkov – friend of the Muses, protector of orphans,
> Who, having brought forth the fruit of immortal works
> From a gentle heart, withered like a tree that has lost its strength.
> But where is the reward? In the other world... Here all is a dream, all is perishable.[10]

About his protection of orphans we know nothing, but we have certainly plenty of evidence to vouch for the fact that he devoted a large part of his productive life to the service of the Muses, even though Thalia at least proved an ungrateful and sometimes deceitful mistress.

[10] A photograph of the plaque, evidently designed for Čulkov's grave, appears in *Literaturnoe Nasledstvo*, Nos. 9-10 (Moscow-Leningrad, 1933), p. 227. See the Frontispiece of the present volume.

BIBLIOGRAPHY

WORKS OF M. D. ČULKOV IN CHRONOLOGICAL ORDER

a. *Eighteenth-century Editions*

Peresmešnik, ili Slavenskie skazki, 4 parts (St. Petersburg, 1766-1768).
—, 2nd ed. (Moscow, 1783-1784).
—, 3rd ed. rev. 5 parts (Moscow, 1789).
Kratkoj mifologičeskoj leksikon (St. Petersburg, 1767).
Poxoždenie Axillesovo pod imjanem Pirry do osady trojanskija (St. Petersburg, 1769).
—, 2nd ed. (Moscow, 1788).
I to i së (St. Petersburg, 1769).
Parnasskij ščepetil'nik (St. Petersburg, 1770).
Prigožaja povarixa, ili poxoždenie razvratnoj ženščiny, Part I (St. Petersburg, 1770).
Sobranie raznyx pesen, 4 parts (St. Petersburg, 1770-1774).
—, 2nd ed. (St. Petersburg, 1776).
Novoe i polnoe sobranie rossijskix pesen, 3rd ed. enlarged, 6 parts (Moscow, 1780-1781).
—, 4th ed. (Moscow, 1788).
Plačevnoe padenie stixotvorcev (St. Petersburg, 1775).
Istoričeskoe opisanie rossijskoj kommercii pri vsex portax i granicax ot drevnix vremjan do nyne nastojaščego i vsex preimuščestvennyx uzakonenij po onoj Gosudarja Imperatora Petra velikogo i nyne blagopolučno carstvujuščej Gosudaryni Imperatricy Ekateriny velikija, 7 vols. (St. Petersburg and Moscow, 1781-1788).
Slovar' russkix sueverij (St. Petersburg, 1782).
Abevega russkix sueverij (Moscow, 1786).
Istorija (kratkaja) rossijskoj torgovli (Moscow, 1788).
Slovar' učreždënnyx v Rossii jarmarok, izdannyj dlja obraščajuščixsja v torgovle (Moscow, 1788).
Ekonomičeskie zapiski dlja vsegdašnego ispolnenija v derevnjax prikazčiku i račitel'nomu èkonomu (Moscow, 1788).
—, 2nd ed. enlarged (Moscow, 1790).
Lečebnik sel'skij, ili slovar', vračevanija boleznej byvaemyx v rode čelovečeskom, tak že v rode skockom i ptic domašnix, 5 parts (Moscow, 1789-1790).
Nastavlenie neobxodimo nužnoe dlja rossijskix kupcov, a bolee dlja molodyx ljudej, soderžaščee pravila buxgalterii (Moscow, 1791).
Slovar' juridičeskij, ili svod rossijskix uzakonenij, vremjannyx učreždenij, suda i raspravy, 5 parts (Moscow, 1792-1796).

b. *Modern Editions*

Three burlesque poems from *I to i së* in *Russkaja poèzija*, I: *XVIII vek. Èpoxa klassicizma*, ed. S. A. Vengerov (St. Petersburg, 1897); in *Iroi-komičeskaja poèma*, ed. B. Tomaševskij (Leningrad, 1933); and in *Poèty XVIII veka*, ed. G. P. Makogonenko and I. Z. Serman, I (Leningrad, 1958).
Prigožaja povarixa in V. L. Burcev, *Obstojatel'noe bibliografičeskoe opisanie*, V (St. Petersburg, 1901); in *Prigožaja povarixa*, ed. A. A. Titov (Moscow, 1904); and in *Russkaja proza XVIII veka*, ed. A. V. Zapadov and G. P. Makogonenko, I (Leningrad, 1950). The last edition also contains parts of *Peresmešnik*.
Sobranie raznyx pesen in *Sočinenija Mixaila Dmitrieviča Čulkova*, I (St. Petersburg, 1913).
"Kak xočeš' nazovi" (Čulkov's hitherto unpublished play) in *Literaturnoe nasledstvo*, Nos. 9-10 (Moscow-Leningrad, 1933).

SELECTED BIBLIOGRAPHY

Adam, Antoine, *Histoire de la littérature française au 17-e siècle*, 5 vols. (Paris, 1948-56).
Adrianova-Peretc, V. P., *Russkaja demokratičeskaja satira XVII veka* (Moscow-Leningrad, 1954).
Auerbach, Erich, *Mimesis* (Princeton, 1953).
Bar, F., *Le genre burlesque* (Paris, 1960).
Belozerskaja, N., *Vasilij Trofimovič Narežnyj. Istoriko-literaturnyj očerk*, 2nd ed. (St. Petersburg, 1896).
Berkov, P. N., *Istorija russkoj žurnalistiki XVIII veka* (Moscow-Leningrad, 1952).
——, "Ivan Šiškin – literaturnyj dejatel' 1740-kh godov (K istorii russkogo romana: ot rukopisnoj povesti k pečatnomu romanu"), in *Voprosy izučenija russkoj literatury XI-XX vekov* (Moscow-Leningrad, 1958), pp. 49-63.
Bolotov, A. I., "Mysli i bespristrastnye suždenija o romanax", *Literaturnoe nasledstvo*, Nos. 9-10 (Moscow-Leningrad, 1933).
Booth, Wayne C., *The Rhetoric of Fiction* (Chicago, 1961).
Brang, Peter, *Studien zu Theorie und Praxis der russischen Erzählung: 1770-1811* (Wiesbaden, 1960).
Bulič, N., *Sumarokov i sovremennaja emu kritika* (St. Petersburg, 1854).
Burgess, M., "Fairs and Entertainers in 18th Century Russia", *Slavonic and East European Review*, XXXVIII (December, 1959), 95-113.
Catherine II, Empress of Russia, *Vsjakaja vsjačina* (St. Petersburg, 1769-1770).
Dmitriev, M. A., *Meloči iz zapasa moej pamjati*, 2nd ed. (Moscow, 1869).
Evgenij (Metropolitan), *Slovar' russkix sveckix pisatelej, sootečestvennikov i čužestrancev, pisavšix v Rossii* (Moscow, 1845).
Èmin, Fëdor, *Adskaja počta* (St. Petersburg, 1769).
——, *Nepostojannaja Fortuna, ili poxoždenie Miramonda* (St. Petersburg, 1763).
Fomin, A., "K biografii M. D. Čulkova (Rod. 1740 g-um. 1793 g.)", *Knigovedenie*, Nos. 7-8 (1894), p. 16.
Gimbutas, Marija, "Ancient Slavic Religion: A Synopsis", *To Honor Roman Jakobson*, I (Mouton, The Hague-Paris, 1967), 738-759.
Green, F. C., *French Novelists, Manners and Ideas* (New York, 1929).
Gric, T., Trenin, V., Nikitin, M., *Slovesnost' i kommercija* (Knižnaja lavka A. F. Smirdina) (Moscow, 1929).

Gudzij, N. K., ed., *Xrestomatija po drevnej russkoj literature XI-XVII vekov*, 5th ed. (Moscow, 1952).
Gukovskij, G. A., *Očerki po istorii russkoj literatury XVIII veka: dvorjanskaja fronda v literature 1750-x–1760-x godov* (Moscow, 1936).
—, *Očerki po istorii russkoj literatury i obščestvennoj mysli XVIII veka* (Leningrad, 1938).
—, "Èmin i Sumarokov", *XVIII Vek*, No. 2 Moscow-Leningrad, 1940), 77-94.
Inozemcev, I., "Spravočnye knigi XVIII veka (Perevodnye leksikony - M. D. Čulkov i ego slovari)", *Antikvar*, Nos, 9-12 (1903), pp. 105-107.
Istorija russkogo romana, ed. G. M. Fridlender, I (Moscow-Leningrad, 1962).
Kožinov, V., *Proisxoždenie romana: teoretiko-istoričeskij očerk* (Moscow, 1963).
Kuz'mina, V. D., *Rycarskij roman na Rusi* (Moscow, 1964).
Longinov, M. N., "Neskol'ko zametok dlja istorii russkogo teatra i dlja biografii nekotoryx starinnyx russkix aktërov", *Russkij Arxiv*, No. 7 (1870), pp. 1348-1366.
—, "O romane *Prigožaja povarixa* (1770)", *Sovremennik*, No. 7 (1856), pp. 19-21.
Lotman, J., "Die Entwicklungswege des Romans in der russischen Literatur des 18. Jahrhunderts", in *Studien zur Geschichte der russischen Literatur des 18. Jahrhunderts*, ed. H. Grasshoff and U. Lehmann (Berlin, 1963), pp. 22-51.
Lukin, V., *Sočinenija i perevody* (St. Petersburg, 1765).
Majkov, V., *Igrok lombera* (St. Petersburg, 1763).
Majkov, L. N., *Očerki po istorii literatury XVII i XVIII stoletij* (St. Petersburg, 1889).
Mathauserová, S., "Der Roman des russischen Schriftstellers M. D. Čulkov", *Studien zur Geschichte der russischen Literatur des 18. Jahrhunderts* (Berlin, 1963), 96-103.
—, *Ruský zdroj monologické románové formy: M. D. Čulkov* (Prague, 1961).
Mečnikova, E., "Na zare russkogo romana", *Golos minuvšego*, No. 6 (1914), pp. 5-40.
Mesjaceva, G. I., *Satiričeskie žurnaly M. D. Čulkova i F. A. Èmina. Avtoreferat diss.* (Moscow, 1953).
Meynieux, André, *La littérature et le métier d'écrivain en Russie avant Pouchkine* (Paris, 1966).
Moiseeva, G. N., *Russkie povesti pervoj treti XVIII veka* (Moscow-Leningrad, 1965).
Morillot, Paul, *Scarron et le genre burlesque* (Paris, 1888).
"Nachricht von einigen russischen Schriftstellern, nebst einem kurzen Berichte vom russischen Theater", in *Materialy dlja istorii russkoj literatury*, ed. P. A. Efremov (St. Petersburg, 1867).
Nečaeva, V., "Russkij bytovoj roman XVIII veka. M. D. Čulkov", *Učënye zapiski. RANION*, Vol. 2, (1928), 5-41.
Neustroev, A. N., *Istoričeskoe rozyskanie o russkix povremennyx izdanijax i sbornikax za 1703-1802 gg.* (St. Petersburg, 1874).
—, *Ukazatel' k russkim povremennym izdateljam i sbornikam za 1703-1802 gg. i k istoričeskomu rozyskaniju o nix* (St. Petersburg, 1898).
Novikov, N., *Opyt istoričeskogo slovarja o rossijskix pisateljax* (St. Petersburg, 1772).
—, *Truten'* (St. Petersburg, 1769-1770).
Orlov, P. A., "Real'no-bytovye romany Čulkova i ego satiriko-bytovye povesti", *Učënye zapiski Rjazan'skogo gos. ped. instituta*, No. 8 (1949), pp. 60-97.
Popov, M., *Dosugi, ili Sobranie sočinenij i perevodov*, 2 vols. (St. Petersburg, 1772).
Prikazčikova, E. V., "Ideolog kupečestva M. D. Čulkov", in *Istorija russkoj*

èkonomičeskoj mysli, ed. A. I. Paškov, I (Moscow, 1955), pp. 490-518.

Putilov, V. N., "O žurnalax Čulkova (*I to i së i Parnasskij ščepetil'nik*)", *Učënye zapiski Leningradskogo gos. ped. instituta im. A. I. Gercena*, Vol. 29 (1940), 87-112.

Pypin, A. N., "Izučenie russkoj narodnosti. Ponjatija o narodnosti v XVIII veke", *Vestnik Evropy*, No. 11 (1881), 340-350.

Raeff, Marc, *Origins of the Russian Intelligentsia: The Eighteenth-Century Nobility* (New York, 1966).

Rogger, Hans, *The Development of the Russian National Consciousness in the Eighteenth Century* (Cambridge, Mass., 1960).

Romanciers du 17-e siècle, ed. Antoine Adam (Paris, Pléiade, 1958).

Russkie satiričeskie žurnaly XVIII veka: izbrannye stat'i i zametki, comp. L. B. Lextblau (Moscow, 1940).

Saintsbury, George, *A History of the French Novel*, I (London, 1917).

Scarron, Paul, *Le Romant Comique*, ed. Henri Bénac, 2 vols. (Paris, 1951).

Semennikov, V. P., *Materialy dlja istorii russkoj literatury i dlja slovarja pisatelej èpoxi Ekateriny II* (St. Petersburg, 1914).

—, *Russkie satiričeskie žurnaly 1769 – 1774 gg. Rozyskanija ob izdateljax ix i sotrudnikax* (St. Petersburg, 1914).

Serman, I. Z., "Stanovlenie i razvitie romana v russkoj literature serediny XVIII veka", in *Iz istorii russkix literaturnyx otnošenij XVIII-XX vekov* (Moscow-Leningrad, 1959), pp. 82-95.

Sipovskij, V. V., *Očerki po istorii russkogo romana* (St. Petersburg, 1909).

Šklovskij, V., *Čulkov i Levšin* (Leningrad, 1933).

—, *O teorii prozy* (Moscow-Leningrad, 1925).

Štrange, M. M., *Demokratičeskaja intelligencija Rossii v XVIII veka* (Moscow, 1965).

Striedter, Jurij, *Der Schelmenroman in Russland: ein Beitrag zur Geschichte des russischen Romans vor Gogol'* (Berlin, 1961).

Sumarokov, A. P., *Izbrannye proizvedenija*, 2nd ed. (Leningrad, 1957).

—, *Trudoljubivaja pčela* (St. Petersburg, 1759).

Svetlov, L., "M. D. Čulkov – avtor pamfleta *Žizn' nekotorogo muža*", *Russkaja literatura*, No. 2 (1963), pp. 188-197.

Svodnyj katalog russkoj knigi graždanskoj pečati XVIII veka, 5 vols. (Moscow, 1963-67).

Tixonravov, N. S., *Sočinenija*, 3 vols. (Moscow, 1898).

Valentinova, I. A., "Leksika xudožestvennoj prozy M. D. Čulkova", *Učënye zapiski Čitinskogo gos. ped. instituta*, No. 3 (1958), pp. 217-316.

—, "Prostorečnaja leksika i eë ispol'zovanie v literaturnom jazyke II poloviny XVIII veka (Na materiale xudožestvennoj prozy M. D. Čulkova", in *Sbornik referatov dokladov nauč. konferencii* (Chita, 1959), pp. 126-138.

F. G. Volkov i russkij teatr ego vremeni. Sbornik materialov, ed. Ju. A. Dmitriev (Moscow, 1953).

Vsevolodskij-Gerngross, V., *Russkij teatr. Ot istokov do serediny XVIII veka* (Moscow, 1957).

—, *Russkij teatr vtoroj poloviny XVIII veka* (Moscow, 1960).

Watt, Ian, *The Rise of the Novel* (Los Angeles and Berkeley, 1962).

Widnäs, M., "La Constitution du Fonds Slave de la Bibliothèque de Helsinki", *Cahiers du monde russe et soviétique*, II (Paris, 1961), 395-408.

Worcester, David, *Art of Satire* (Cambridge, Mass., 1940).

"Xronika russkogo teatra", *Čtenija v imp. Obščestve istorii i drevnostej rossijskix pri Mosk. universitete*, Vols. 121 and 122 (1882).

Zapadov, A. V., "Žurnal M. D. Čulkova *I to i së* i ego literaturnoe okruženie", in *XVIII Vek*, No. 2 (Moscow-Leningrad, 1940), pp. 95-141.
"Zapiski Aleksandra Mixajloviča Turgeneva", *Russkaja starina*, Vol. 53 (1887), 102-104.

INDEX